Getting to

Getting to YES

Negotiating Agreement Without Giving In

Roger Fisher and William Ury
with Bruce Patton, editor

ARROW

Arrow Books Limited
20 Vauxhall Bridge Road, London SW1V 2SA

An imprint of Random House Ltd

London Melbourne Sydney Auckland Johannesburg
and agencies throughout the world

First published in Great Britain by Hutchinson 1982
Hutchinson Paperback edition 1983
Business Books edition 1986

Arrow edition 1987
12

Printed and bound in Great Britain by
The Guernsey Press Co Ltd
Guernsey, Channel Islands

ISBN 0 09 951730 2

To our fathers,
Walter T. Fisher and Melvin C. Ury,
who by example taught us
the power of principle

Acknowledgments

This book began as a question: What is the best way for people to deal with their differences? For example, what is the best advice one could give a husband and wife getting divorced who want to know how to reach a fair and mutually satisfactory agreement without ending up in a bitter fight? Perhaps more difficult, what advice would you give *one* of them who wanted to do the same thing? Every day, families, neighbors, couples, employees, bosses, businesses, consumers, salesmen, lawyers, and nations face this same dilemma of how to get to yes without going to war. Drawing on our respective backgrounds in international law and anthropology and an extensive collaboration over the years with practitioners, colleagues, and students, we have evolved a practical method for negotiating agreement amicably without giving in.

We have tried out ideas on lawyers, businessmen, government officials, judges, prison wardens, diplomats, insurance representatives, military officers, coal miners, and oil executives. We gratefully acknowledge those who responded with criticism and with suggestions distilled from their experience. We benefited immensely.

In truth, so many people have contributed so extensively to our learning over the years that it is no longer possible to say precisely to whom we are indebted for which ideas in what form. Those who contributed the most understand that footnotes were omitted not because we think every idea original, but rather to keep the text readable when we owe so much to so many.

We could not fail to mention, however, our debt to Howard Raiffa. His kind but forthright criticism has repeatedly improved the approach, and his notions on seeking joint gains by exploiting differences and using imaginative procedures for settling difficult issues have inspired sections on these subjects. Louis Sohn, deviser and negotiator extraordinaire, was always encouraging, always creative, always looking forward. Among our many debts to him, we owe our introduction to the idea of using a single negotiating text, which we call the One-Text Procedure. And we would like to thank Michael Doyle and David Strauss for their creative ideas on running brainstorming sessions.

Good anecdotes and examples are hard to find. We are greatly indebted to Jim Sebenius for his accounts of the Law of the Sea Conference (as well as for his thoughtful criticism of the method), to Tom Griffith for an account of his negotiation with an insurance adjuster, and to Mary Parker Follett for the story of two men quarreling in a library.

We want especially to thank all those who read this book in various drafts and gave us the benefit of their criticism, including our students in the January Negotiation Workshops of 1980 and 1981 at Harvard Law School, and Frank Sander, John Cooper, and William Lincoln who taught those workshops with us. In particular, we want to thank those members of Harvard's Negotiation Seminar whom we have not already mentioned; they listened to us patiently these last two years and offered many helpful suggestions: John Dunlop, James Healy, David Kuechle, Thomas Schelling, and Lawrence Susskind. To all of our friends and associates we owe more than we can say, but the final responsibility for the content of this book lies with the authors; if the result is not yet perfect, it is not for lack of our colleagues' efforts.

Without family and friends, writing would be intolerable. For moral support (and constructive criticism) we thank Caroline Fisher, David Lax, Frances Turnbull, and Janice Ury.

Without Francis Fisher this book would never have been written. He had the felicity of introducing the two of us some four years ago.

Finer secretarial help we could not have had. Thanks to Deborah Reimel for her unfailing competence, moral support, and firm but gracious reminders, and to Denise Trybula, who never wavered in her diligence and cheerfulness. And special thanks to the people at Word Processing, led by Cynthia Smith, who met the test of an endless series of drafts and near impossible deadlines.

Then there are our editors. By reorganizing and cutting this book in half, Marty Linsky made it far more readable. To spare our readers, he had the good sense not to spare our feelings. Thanks also to Peter Kinder, June Kinoshita, and Bob Ross. June struggled to make the language less sexist. Where we have not succeeded, we apologize to those who may be offended. We also want to thank Julian Bach, our agent, and Dick McAdoo and his associates at Houghton Mifflin who made the production of this book both possible and pleasurable.

Finally, we want to thank Bruce Patton, our friend and colleague, editor and mediator. No one has contributed more to this book. From the very beginning he helped brainstorm and organize the syllogism of the book. He has reorganized almost every chapter and edited every word. If books were movies, this would be known as a Patton Production.

Roger Fisher
William Ury

Contents

Introduction

Like it or not, you are a negotiator. Negotiation is a fact of life. You discuss a raise with your boss. You try to agree with a stranger on a price for his house. Two lawyers try to settle a lawsuit arising from a car accident. A group of oil companies plan a joint venture exploring for offshore oil. A city official meets with union leaders to avert a transit strike. The United States Secretary of State sits down with his Soviet counterpart to seek an agreement limiting nuclear arms. All these are negotiations.

Everyone negotiates something every day. Like Molière's Monsieur Jourdain, who was delighted to learn that he had been speaking prose all his life, people negotiate even when they don't think of themselves as doing so. A person negotiates with his spouse about where to go for dinner and with his child about when the lights go out. Negotiation is a basic means of getting what you want from others. It is back-and-forth communication designed to reach an agreement when you and the other side have some interests that are shared and others that are opposed.

More and more occasions require negotiation; conflict is a growth industry. Everyone wants to participate in decisions that affect them; fewer and fewer people will accept decisions dictated by someone else. People differ, and they use negotiation to handle their differences. Whether in business, government, or the family, people reach most decisions through negotiation. Even when they go to court, they almost always negotiate a settlement before trial.

Although negotiation takes place every day, it is not easy to do well. Standard strategies for negotiation often leave people dissatisfied, worn out, or alienated — and frequently all three.

People find themselves in a dilemma. They see two ways to negotiate: soft or hard. The soft negotiator wants to avoid personal conflict and so makes concessions readily in order to reach agreement. He wants an amicable resolution; yet he often ends up exploited and feeling bitter. The hard negotiator sees any situation as a contest of wills in which the side that takes the more extreme positions and holds out longer fares better. He wants to win; yet he often ends up producing an equally hard response which exhausts him and his resources and harms his relationship with the other side. Other standard negotiating strategies fall between hard and soft, but each involves an attempted trade-off between getting what you want and getting along with people.

There is a third way to negotiate, a way neither hard nor soft, but rather both hard *and* soft. The method of *principled negotiation* developed at the Harvard Negotiation Project is to decide issues on their merits rather than through a haggling process focused on what each side says it will and won't do. It suggests that you look for mutual gains wherever possible, and that where your interests conflict, you should insist that the result be based on some fair standards independent of the will of either side. The method of principled negotiation is hard on the merits, soft on the people. It employs no tricks and no posturing. Principled negotiation shows you how to obtain what you are entitled to and still be decent. It enables you to be fair while protecting you against those who would take advantage of your fairness.

This book is about the method of principled negotiation. The first chapter describes problems that arise in using the standard strategies of positional bargaining. The next four chapters lay out the four principles of the method. The last three chapters answer the questions most commonly asked about the method: What if the other side is more powerful? What if they will not play along? And what if they use dirty tricks?

Principled negotiation can be used by United States diplomats in arms control talks with the Soviet Union, by Wall Street lawyers representing Fortune 500 companies in antitrust cases, and by couples in deciding everything from where to go for vacation to how to divide their property if they get divorced. Anyone can use this method.

Every negotiation is different, but the basic elements do not change. Principled negotiation can be used whether there is one issue or several; two parties or many; whether there is a prescribed ritual, as in collective bargaining, or an impromptu free-for-all, as in talking with hijackers. The method applies whether the other side is more experienced or less, a hard bargainer or a friendly one. Principled negotiation is an all-purpose strategy. Unlike almost all other strategies, if the other side learns this one, it does not become more difficult to use; it becomes easier. If they read this book, all the better.

I | The Problem

1. Don't Bargain Over Positions

1 | Don't Bargain Over Positions

Whether a negotiation concerns a contract, a family quarrel, or a peace settlement among nations, people routinely engage in positional bargaining. Each side takes a position, argues for it, and makes concessions to reach a compromise. The classic example of this negotiating minuet is the haggling that takes place between a customer and the proprietor of a secondhand store:

CUSTOMER	SHOPKEEPER
How much do you want for this brass dish?	
	That is a beautiful antique, isn't it? I guess I could let it go for $75.
Oh come on, it's dented. I'll give you $15.	
	Really! I might consider a serious offer, but $15 certainly isn't serious.
Well, I could go to $20, but I would never pay anything like $75. Quote me a realistic price.	
	You drive a hard bargain, young lady. $60 cash, right now.

CUSTOMER	SHOPKEEPER
$25.	
	It cost me a great deal more than that. Make me a *serious* offer.
$37.50. That's the highest I will go.	
	Have you noticed the engraving on that dish? Next year pieces like that will be worth twice what you pay today.

And so it goes, on and on. Perhaps they will reach agreement; perhaps not.

Any method of negotiation may be fairly judged by three criteria: It should produce a wise agreement if agreement is possible. It should be efficient. And it should improve or at least not damage the relationship between the parties. (A wise agreement can be defined as one which meets the legitimate interests of each side to the extent possible, resolves conflicting interests fairly, is durable, and takes community interests into account.)

The most common form of negotiation, illustrated by the above example, depends upon successively taking — and then giving up — a sequence of positions.

Taking positions, as the customer and storekeeper do, serves some useful purposes in a negotiation. It tells the other side what you want; it provides an anchor in an uncertain and pressured situation; and it can eventually produce the terms of an acceptable agreement. But those purposes can be served in other ways. And positional bargaining fails to meet the basic criteria of producing a wise agreement, efficiently and amicably.

Arguing over positions produces unwise agreements

When negotiators bargain over positions, they tend to lock themselves into those positions. The more you clarify your position and defend it against attack, the more committed you become to it. The more you try to convince the other side of the impossibility of changing your opening position, the more difficult it becomes to do so. Your ego becomes identified with your position. You now have a new interest in "saving face" — in reconciling future action with past positions — making it less and less likely that any agreement will wisely reconcile the parties' original interests.

The danger that positional bargaining will impede a negotiation was well illustrated by the breakdown of the talks under President Kennedy for a comprehensive ban on nuclear testing. A critical question arose: How many on-site inspections per year should the Soviet Union and the United States be permitted to make within the other's territory to investigate suspicious seismic events? The Soviet Union finally agreed to three inspections. The United States insisted on no less than ten. And there the talks broke down — over positions — despite the fact that no one understood whether an "inspection" would involve one person looking around for one day, or a hundred people prying indiscriminately for a month. The parties had made little attempt to design an inspection procedure that would reconcile the United States's interest in verification with the desire of both countries for minimal intrusion.

As more attention is paid to positions, less attention is devoted to meeting the underlying concerns of the parties. Agreement becomes less likely. Any agreement reached may reflect a mechanical splitting of the difference between final positions rather than a solution carefully crafted to meet the legitimate interests of the parties. The result is frequently an agreement less satisfactory to each side than it could have been.

Arguing over positions is inefficient

The standard method of negotiation may produce either agreement, as with the price of a brass dish, or breakdown, as with the number of on-site inspections. In either event, the process takes a lot of time.

Bargaining over positions creates incentives that stall settlement. In positional bargaining you try to improve the chance that any settlement reached is favorable to you by starting with an extreme position, by stubbornly holding to it, by deceiving the other party as to your true views, and by making small concessions only as necessary to keep the negotiation going. The same is true for the other side. Each of those factors tends to interfere with reaching a settlement promptly. The more extreme the opening positions and the smaller the concessions, the more time and effort it will take to discover whether or not agreement is possible.

The standard minuet also requires a large number of individual decisions as each negotiator decides what to offer, what to reject, and how much of a concession to make. Decision-making is difficult and time-consuming at best. Where each decision not only involves yielding to the other side but will likely produce pressure to yield further, a negotiator has little incentive to move quickly. Dragging one's feet, threatening to walk out, stonewalling, and other such tactics become commonplace. They all increase the time and costs of reaching agreement as well as the risk that no agreement will be reached at all.

Arguing over positions endangers an ongoing relationship

Positional bargaining becomes a contest of will. Each negotiator asserts what he will and won't do. The task of jointly devising an acceptable solution tends to become a battle. Each side tries through sheer will power to force the other to change its position. "I'm not going to give in. If you want to go to the movies with me, it's *The Maltese Falcon* or nothing." Anger and resentment often result as one side sees itself bending to the rigid will of the other while its own legitimate concerns go unaddressed. Positional bargaining thus strains and sometimes shatters the relationship between the parties. Commercial enterprises that have been doing business together for years may part company. Neighbors may stop speaking to each other. Bitter feelings generated by one such encounter may last a lifetime.

When there are many parties, positional bargaining is even worse

Although it is convenient to discuss negotiation in terms of two persons, you and "the other side," in fact, almost every negotiation involves more than two persons. Several different parties may sit at the table, or each side may have constituents, higher-ups, boards of directors, or committees with whom they must deal. The more people involved in a negotiation, the more serious the drawbacks to positional bargaining.

If some 150 countries are negotiating, as in various United Nations conferences, positional bargaining is next to impossible. It may take all to say yes, but only one to say no. Reciprocal concessions are difficult: to whom do you make a concession? Yet even thousands of bilateral deals would still fall short of a multilateral agreement. In such situations, positional bargaining leads to the formation of coalitions among parties whose shared interests are often more symbolic than substantive. At the United Nations, such coalitions produce negotiations between "the" North and "the" South, or between "the" East and "the" West. Because there are many members in a group, it becomes more difficult to develop a common position. What is worse, once they have painfully developed and agreed upon a position, it becomes much harder to change it. Altering a position proves equally difficult when additional participants are higher authorities who, while absent from the table, must nevertheless give their approval.

Being nice is no answer

Many people recognize the high costs of hard positional bargaining, particularly on the parties and their relationship. They hope to avoid them by following a more gentle style of negotiation. Instead of seeing the other side as adversaries, they prefer to see them as friends. Rather than emphasizing a goal of victory, they emphasize the necessity of reaching agreement. In a soft negotiating game the standard moves are to make offers and concessions, to trust the other side, to be friendly, and to yield as necessary to avoid confrontation.

The following table illustrates two styles of positional bargaining, soft and hard. Most people see their choice of negotiating strategies as between these two styles. Looking at the table as presenting a choice, should you be a soft or a hard positional bargainer? Or should you perhaps follow a strategy somewhere in between?

The soft negotiating game emphasizes the importance of building and maintaining a relationship. Within families and among friends much negotiation takes place in this way. The process tends to be efficient, at least to the extent of producing results quickly. As each party competes with the other in being more generous and more forthcoming, an agreement becomes highly likely. But it may not be a wise one. The results may not be as tragic as in the O. Henry story about an impoverished couple in which the loving wife sells her hair in order to buy a handsome chain for her husband's watch, and the unknowing husband sells his watch in order to buy beautiful combs for his wife's hair. However, any negotiation primarily concerned with the relationship runs the risk of producing a sloppy agreement.

More seriously, pursuing a soft and friendly form of posi-

PROBLEM

Positional Bargaining: Which Game Should You Play?

SOFT	HARD
Participants are friends.	Participants are adversaries.
The goal is agreement.	The goal is victory.
Make concessions to cultivate the relationship.	Demand concessions as a condition of the relationship.
Be soft on the people and the problem.	Be hard on the problem and the people.
Trust others.	Distrust others.
Change your position easily.	Dig in to your position.
Make offers.	Make threats.
Disclose your bottom line.	Mislead as to your bottom line.
Accept one-sided losses to reach agreement.	Demand one-sided gains as the price of agreement.
Search for the single answer: the one *they* will accept.	Search for the single answer: the one *you* will accept.
Insist on agreement.	Insist on your position.
Try to avoid a contest of will.	Try to win a contest of will.
Yield to pressure.	Apply pressure.

tional bargaining makes you vulnerable to someone who plays a hard game of positional bargaining. In positional bargaining, a hard game dominates a soft one. If the hard bargainer insists on concessions and makes threats while the soft bargainer yields in order to avoid confrontation and insists on agreement, the negotiating game is biased in favor of the hard player. The process will produce an agreement, although it may not be a wise one. It will certainly be more favorable to the hard positional bargainer than to the soft one. If your response to sustained, hard positional bargaining is soft positional bargaining, you will probably lose your shirt.

There is an alternative

If you do not like the choice between hard and soft positional bargaining, you can change the game.

The game of negotiation takes place at two levels. At one level, negotiation addresses the substance; at another, it focuses — usually implicitly — on the procedure for dealing with the substance. The first negotiation may concern your salary, the terms of a lease, or a price to be paid. The second negotiation concerns how you will negotiate the substantive question: by soft positional bargaining, by hard positional bargaining, or by some other method. This second negotiation is a game about a game — a "meta-game." Each move you make within a negotiation is not only a move that deals with rent, salary, or other substantive questions; it also helps structure the rules of the game you are playing. Your move may serve to keep the negotiations within an ongoing mode, or it may constitute a game-changing move.

This second negotiation by and large escapes notice because it seems to occur without conscious decision. Only when dealing with someone from another country, particularly someone with a markedly different cultural background, are you likely to see the necessity of establishing some accepted process for the substantive negotiations. But whether consciously or not, you are negotiating procedural rules with every move you make, even if those moves appear exclusively concerned with substance.

The answer to the question of whether to use soft positional bargaining or hard is "neither." Change the game. At the Harvard Negotiation Project we have been developing an alternative to positional bargaining: a method of negotiation explicitly designed to produce wise outcomes efficiently and amicably. This method, called *principled negotiation* or *negotiation on the merits,* can be boiled down to four basic points.

These four points define a straightforward method of negotiation that can be used under almost any circumstance. Each point deals with a basic element of negotiation, and suggests what you should do about it.

People: Separate the people from the problem.

Interests: Focus on interests, not positions.

Options: Generate a variety of possibilities before deciding what to do.

Criteria: Insist that the result be based on some objective standard.

The first point responds to the fact that human beings are not computers. We are creatures of strong emotions who often have radically different perceptions and have difficulty communicating clearly. Emotions typically become entangled with the objective merits of the problem. Taking positions just makes this worse because people's egos become identified with their positions. Hence, before working on the substantive problem, the "people problem" should be disentangled from it and dealt with separately. Figuratively if not literally, the participants should come to see themselves as working side by side, attacking the problem, not each other. Hence the first proposition: *Separate the people from the problem.*

The second point is designed to overcome the drawback of focusing on people's stated positions when the object of a negotiation is to satisfy their underlying interests. A negotiating position often obscures what you really want. Compromising between positions is not likely to produce an agreement which will effectively take care of the human needs that led people to adopt those positions. The second basic element of the method is: *Focus on interests, not positions.*

The third point responds to the difficulty of designing optimal solutions while under pressure. Trying to decide in the presence of an adversary narrows your vision. Having a lot at stake inhibits creativity. So does searching for the one right solution. You can offset these constraints by setting aside a designated time within which to think up a wide range of possible solutions that advance shared interests and creatively reconcile differing interests. Hence the third basic point: Before trying to reach agreement, *invent options for mutual gain*.

Where interests are directly opposed, a negotiator may be able to obtain a favorable result simply by being stubborn. That method tends to reward intransigence and produce arbitrary results. However, you can counter such a negotiator by insisting that his single say-so is not enough and that the agreement must reflect some fair standard independent of the naked will of either side. This does not mean insisting that the terms be based on the standard you select, but only that some fair standard such as market value, expert opinion, custom, or law determine the outcome. By discussing such criteria rather than what the parties are willing or unwilling to do, neither party need give in to the other; both can defer to a fair solution. Hence the fourth basic point: *Insist on objective criteria*.

The method of principled negotiation is contrasted with hard and soft positional bargaining in the table below, which shows the four basic points of the method in boldface type.

The four basic propositions of principled negotiation are relevant from the time you begin to think about negotiating until the time either an agreement is reached or you decide to break off the effort. That period can be divided into three stages: analysis, planning, and discussion.

During the *analysis* stage you are simply trying to diagnose the situation — to gather information, organize it, and think about it. You will want to consider the people problems of partisan perceptions, hostile emotions, and unclear communication, as well as to identify your interests and those of

PROBLEM Positional Bargaining: Which Game Should You Play?		SOLUTION Change the Game — Negotiate on the Merits
SOFT	**HARD**	**PRINCIPLED**
Participants are friends.	Participants are adversaries.	Participants are problem-solvers.
The goal is agreement.	The goal is victory.	The goal is a wise outcome reached efficiently and amicably.
Make concessions to cultivate the relationship.	Demand concessions as a condition of the relationship.	**Separate the people from the problem.**
Be soft on the people and the problem.	Be hard on the problem and the people.	Be soft on the people, hard on the problem.
Trust others.	Distrust others.	Proceed independent of trust.
Change your position easily.	Dig in to your position.	**Focus on interests, not positions.**
Make offers.	Make threats.	Explore interests.
Disclose your bottom line.	Mislead as to your bottom line.	Avoid having a bottom line.
Accept one-sided losses to reach agreement.	Demand one-sided gains as the price of agreement.	**Invent options for mutual gain.**
Search for the single answer: the one *they* will accept.	Search for the single answer: the one *you* will accept.	Develop multiple options to choose from; decide later.
Insist on agreement.	Insist on your position.	**Insist on objective criteria.**
Try to avoid a contest of will.	Try to win a contest of will.	Try to reach a result based on standards independent of will.
Yield to pressure.	Apply pressure.	Reason and be open to reasons; yield to principle, not pressure.

the other side. You will want to note options already on the table and identify any criteria already suggested as a basis for agreement.

During the *planning* stage you deal with the same four elements a second time, both generating ideas and deciding what to do. How do you propose to handle the people problems? Of your interests, which are most important? And what are some realistic objectives? You will want to generate additional options and additional criteria for deciding among them.

Again during the *discussion* stage, when the parties communicate back and forth, looking toward agreement, the same four elements are the best subjects to discuss. Differences in perception, feelings of frustration and anger, and difficulties in communication can be acknowledged and addressed. Each side should come to understand the interests of the other. Both can then jointly generate options that are mutually advantageous and seek agreement on objective standards for resolving opposed interests.

To sum up, in contrast to positional bargaining, the principled negotiation method of focusing on basic interests, mutually satisfying options, and fair standards typically results in a *wise* agreement. The method permits you to reach a gradual consensus on a joint decision *efficiently* without all the transactional costs of digging in to positions only to have to dig yourself out of them. And separating the people from the problem allows you to deal directly and empathetically with the other negotiator as a human being, thus making possible an *amicable* agreement.

Each of the next four chapters expands on one of these four basic points. If at any point you become skeptical, you may want to skip ahead briefly and browse in the final three chapters, which respond to questions commonly raised about the method.

II | The Method

2 | Separate the People from the Problem

Everyone knows how hard it is to deal with a problem without people misunderstanding each other, getting angry or upset, and taking things personally.

A union leader says to his men, "All right, who called the walkout?"

Jones steps forward. "I did. It was that bum foreman Campbell again. That was the fifth time in two weeks he sent me out of our group as a replacement. He's got it in for me, and I'm tired of it. Why should I get all the dirty work?"

Later the union leader confronts Campbell. "Why do you keep picking on Jones? He says you've put him on replacement detail five times in two weeks. What's going on?"

Campbell replies, "I pick Jones because he's the best. I know I can trust him to keep things from fouling up in a group without its point man. I send him on replacement only when it's a key man missing, otherwise I send Smith or someone else. It's just that with the flu going around there've been a lot of point men out. I never knew Jones objected. I thought he liked the responsibility."

In another real-life situation, an insurance company lawyer says to the state insurance commissioner:

"I appreciate your time, Commissioner Thompson. What I'd like to talk to you about is some of the problems we've been having with the presumption clause of the strict-liability regulations. Basically, we think the way the clause was written causes it to have an unfair impact on those insurers whose existing policies contain rate adjustment limitations, and we would like to consider ways it might be revised ——"

The Commissioner, interrupting: "Mr. Johnson, your company had ample opportunity to voice any objection it had during the hearings my department held on those regulations before they were issued. I ran those hearings, Mr. Johnson. I listened to every word of testimony, and I wrote the final version of the strict-liability provisions personally. Are you saying I made a mistake?"

"No, but ——"

"Are you saying I'm unfair?"

"Certainly not, sir, but I think this provision has had consequences none of us foresaw, and ——"

"Listen, Johnson, I promised the public when I campaigned for this position that I would put an end to killer hair dryers and $5000 bombs disguised as cars. And these regulations have done that.

"Your company made a $50 million profit on its strict-liability policies last year. What kind of fool do you think you can play me for, coming in here talking about 'unfair' regulations and 'unforeseen consequences'? I don't want to hear another word of that. Good day, Mr. Johnson."

Now what? Does the insurance company lawyer press the Commissioner on this point, making him angry and probably not getting anywhere? His company does a lot of business in this state. A good relationship with the Commissioner is important. Should he let the matter rest, then, even though he is convinced that this regulation really is unfair, that its long-term effects are likely to be against the public interest, and that not even the experts foresaw this problem at the time of the original hearings?

What is going on in these cases?

Negotiators are people first

A basic fact about negotiation, easy to forget in corporate and international transactions, is that you are dealing not with abstract representatives of the "other side," but with human beings. They have emotions, deeply held values, and different backgrounds and viewpoints; and they are unpredictable. So are you.

This human aspect of negotiation can be either helpful or disastrous. The process of working out an agreement may produce a psychological commitment to a mutually satisfactory outcome. A working relationship where trust, understanding, respect, and friendship are built up over time can make each new negotiation smoother and more efficient. And people's desire to feel good about themselves, and their concern for what others will think of them, can often make them more sensitive to another negotiator's interests.

On the other hand, people get angry, depressed, fearful, hostile, frustrated, and offended. They have egos that are easily threatened. They see the world from their own personal vantage point, and they frequently confuse their perceptions with reality. Routinely, they fail to interpret what you say in the way you intend and do not mean what you understand them to say. Misunderstanding can reinforce prejudice and lead to reactions that produce counterreactions in a vicious circle; rational exploration of possible solutions becomes impossible and a negotiation fails. The purpose of the game becomes scoring points, confirming negative impressions, and apportioning blame at the expense of the substantive interests of both parties.

Failing to deal with others sensitively as human beings prone to human reactions can be disastrous for a negotiation. Whatever else you are doing at any point during a negotiation, from preparation to follow-up, it is worth asking yourself, "Am I paying enough attention to the people problem?"

Every negotiator has two kinds of interests: in the substance and in the relationship

Every negotiator wants to reach an agreement that satisfies his substantive interests. That is why one negotiates. Beyond that, a negotiator also has an interest in his relationship with the other side. An antiques dealer wants both to make a profit on the sale and to turn the customer into a regular one. At a minimum, a negotiator wants to maintain a working relationship good enough to produce an acceptable agreement if one is possible given each side's interests. Usually, more is at stake. Most negotiations take place in the context of an ongoing relationship where it is important to carry on each negotiation in a way that will help rather than hinder future relations and future negotiations. In fact, with many long-term clients, business partners, family members, fellow professionals, government officials, or foreign nations, the ongoing relationship is far more important than the outcome of any particular negotiation.

The relationship tends to become entangled with the problem. A major consequence of the "people problem" in negotiation is that the parties' relationship tends to become entangled with their discussions of substance. On both the giving and receiving end, we are likely to treat people and problem as one. Within the family, a statement such as "The kitchen is a mess" or "Our bank account is low" may be intended simply to identify a problem, but it is likely to be heard as a personal attack. Anger over a situation may lead you to express anger toward some human being associated with it in your mind. Egos tend to become involved in substantive positions.

Another reason that substantive issues become entangled with psychological ones is that people draw from comments on substance unfounded inferences which they then treat as facts about that person's intentions and attitudes toward them.

Unless we are careful, this process is almost automatic; we are seldom aware that other explanations may be equally valid. Thus in the union example, Jones figured that Campbell, the foreman, had it in for him, while Campbell thought he was complimenting Jones and doing him a favor by giving him responsible assignments.

Positional bargaining puts relationship and substance in conflict. Framing a negotiation as a contest of will over positions aggravates the entangling process. I see your position as a statement of how you would like the negotiation to end; from my point of view it demonstrates how little you care about our relationship. If I take a firm position that you consider unreasonable, you assume that I also think of it as an extreme position; it is easy to conclude that I do not value our relationship — or you — very highly.

Positional bargaining deals with a negotiator's interests both in substance and in a good relationship by trading one off against the other. If what counts in the long run for your company is its relationship with the insurance commissioner, then you will probably let this matter drop. Or, if you care more about a favorable solution than being respected or liked by the other side, you can try to trade relationship for substance. "If you won't go along with me on this point, then so much for you. This will be the last time we meet." Yet giving in on a substantive point may buy no friendship; it may do nothing more than convince the other side that you can be taken for a ride.

Separate the relationship from the substance; deal directly with the people problem

Dealing with a substantive problem and maintaining a good working relationship need not be conflicting goals if the parties are committed and psychologically prepared to treat each separately on its own legitimate merits. Base the relationship on accurate perceptions, clear communication, appropriate emotions, and a forward-looking, purposive outlook. Deal with people problems directly; don't try to solve them with substantive concessions.

To deal with psychological problems, use psychological techniques. Where perceptions are inaccurate, you can look for ways to educate. If emotions run high, you can find ways for each person involved to let off steam. Where misunderstanding exists, you can work to improve communication.

To find your way through the jungle of people problems, it is useful to think in terms of three basic categories: perception, emotion, and communication. The various people problems all fall into one of these three baskets.

In negotiating it is easy to forget that you must deal not only with their people problems, but also with your own. Your anger and frustration may obstruct an agreement beneficial to you. Your perceptions are likely to be one-sided, and you may not be listening or communicating adequately. The techniques which follow apply equally well to your people problems as to those of the other side.

Perception

Understanding the other side's thinking is not simply a useful activity that will help you solve your problem. Their thinking *is* the problem. Whether you are making a deal or settling a dispute, differences are defined by the difference between your thinking and theirs. When two people quarrel, they usually quarrel over an object — both may claim a watch — or over an event — each may contend that the other was at fault in causing an automobile accident. The same goes for nations. Morocco and Algeria quarrel over a section of the Western Sahara; India and Pakistan quarrel over each other's development of nuclear bombs. In such circumstances people tend to

assume that what they need to know more about is the object
or the event. They study the watch or they measure the skid
marks at the scene of the accident. They study the Western
Sahara or the detailed history of nuclear weapons development
in India and Pakistan.

Ultimately, however, conflict lies not in objective reality,
but in people's heads. Truth is simply one more argument —
perhaps a good one, perhaps not — for dealing with the difference. The difference itself exists because it exists in their
thinking. Fears, even if ill-founded, are real fears and need to
be dealt with. Hopes, even if unrealistic, may cause a war.
Facts, even if established, may do nothing to solve the problem. Both parties may agree that one lost the watch and the
other found it, but still disagree over who should get it. It may
finally be established that the auto accident was caused by
the blowout of a tire which had been driven 31,402 miles,
but the parties may dispute who should pay for the damage.
The detailed history and geography of the Western Sahara,
no matter how carefully studied and documented, is not the
stuff with which one puts to rest that kind of territorial dispute. No study of who developed what nuclear devices when
will put to rest the conflict between India and Pakistan.

As useful as looking for objective reality can be, it is ultimately the reality as each side sees it that constitutes the
problem in a negotiation and opens the way to a solution.

Put yourself in their shoes. How you see the world depends
on where you sit. People tend to see what they want to see.
Out of a mass of detailed information, they tend to pick out
and focus on those facts that confirm their prior perceptions
and to disregard or misinterpret those that call their perceptions into question. Each side in a negotiation may see only
the merits of its case, and only the faults of the other side's.

The ability to see the situation as the other side sees it, as
difficult as it may be, is one of the most important skills a

negotiator can possess. It is not enough to know that they see
things differently. If you want to influence them, you also
need to understand empathetically the power of their point of
view and to feel the emotional force with which they believe
in it. It is not enough to study them like beetles under a
microscope; you need to know what it feels like to be a beetle.
To accomplish this task you should be prepared to withhold
judgment for a while as you "try on" their views. They may
well believe that their views are "right" as strongly as you
believe yours are. You may see on the table a glass half full
of cool water. Your spouse may see a dirty, half-empty glass
about to cause a ring on the mahogany finish.

Consider the contrasting perceptions of a tenant and a land-
lady negotiating the renewal of a lease:

TENANT'S PERCEPTIONS	LANDLADY'S PERCEPTIONS
The rent is already too high.	The rent has not been increased for a long time.
With other costs going up, I can't afford to pay more for housing.	With other costs going up, I need more rental income.
The apartment needs painting.	He has given that apartment heavy wear and tear.
I know people who pay less for a comparable apartment.	I know people who pay more for a comparable apartment.
Young people like me can't afford to pay high rents.	Young people like him tend to make noise and to be hard on an apartment.
The rent ought to be low because the neighborhood is rundown.	We landlords should raise rents in order to improve the quality of the neighborhood.
I am a desirable tenant with no dogs or cats.	His hi-fi drives me crazy.

I always pay the rent whenever she asks for it.	He never pays the rent until I ask for it.
She is cold and distant; she never asks me how things are.	I am a considerate person who never intrudes on a tenant's privacy.

Understanding their point of view is not the same as agreeing with it. It is true that a better understanding of their thinking may lead you to revise your own views about the merits of a situation. But that is not a *cost* of understanding their point of view, it is a *benefit*. It allows you to reduce the area of conflict, and it also helps you advance your newly enlightened self-interest.

Don't deduce their intentions from your fears. People tend to assume that whatever they fear, the other side intends to do. Consider this story from the *New York Times* of December 25, 1980: "They met in a bar, where he offered her a ride home. He took her down unfamiliar streets. He said it was a shortcut. He got her home so fast she caught the 10 o'clock news." Why is the ending so surprising? We made an assumption based on our fears.

It is all too easy to fall into the habit of putting the worst interpretation on what the other side says or does. A suspicious interpretation often follows naturally from one's existing perceptions. Moreover, it seems the "safe" thing to do, and it shows spectators how bad the other side really is. But the cost of interpreting whatever they say or do in its most dismal light is that fresh ideas in the direction of agreement are spurned, and subtle changes of position are ignored or rejected.

Don't blame them for your problem. It is tempting to hold the other side responsible for your problem. "Your company is totally unreliable. Every time you service our rotary generator here at the factory, you do a lousy job and it breaks down again." Blaming is an easy mode to fall into, particularly when you feel that the other side is indeed responsible.

But even if blaming is justified, it is usually counterproductive. Under attack, the other side will become defensive and will resist what you have to say. They will cease to listen, or they will strike back with an attack of their own. Assessing blame firmly entangles the people with the problem.

When you talk about the problem, separate the symptoms from the person with whom you are talking. "Our rotary generator that you service has broken down again. That is three times in the last month. The first time it was out of order for an entire week. This factory needs a functioning generator. I want your advice on how we can minimize our risk of generator breakdown. Should we change service companies or what?"

Discuss each other's perceptions. One way to deal with differing perceptions is to make them explicit and discuss them with the other side. As long as you do this in a frank, honest manner without either side blaming the other for the problem as each sees it, such a discussion may provide the understanding they need to take what you say seriously, and vice versa.

It is common in a negotiation to treat as "unimportant" those concerns of the other side perceived as not standing in the way of an agreement. To the contrary, communicating loudly and convincingly things you are willing to say that they would like to hear can be one of the best investments you as a negotiator can make.

Consider the negotiation over the transfer of technology which arose at the Law of the Sea Conference. From 1974 to 1981 some 150 nations gathered together in New York and Geneva to formulate rules to govern uses of the ocean from fishing rights to mining manganese in the deep seabed. At one point, representatives of the developing countries expressed keen interest in an exchange of technology; their countries wanted to be able to acquire from the highly industrialized nations advanced technical knowledge and equipment for deep-seabed mining.

The United States and other developed countries saw no difficulty in satisfying that desire — and therefore saw the issue of technology transfer as unimportant. In one sense it was unimportant to them, but it was a great mistake for them to *treat* the subject as unimportant. By devoting substantial time to working out the practical arrangements for transferring technology, they might have made their offer far more credible and far more attractive to the developing countries. By dismissing the issue as a matter of lesser importance to be dealt with later, the industrialized states gave up a low-cost opportunity to provide the developing countries with an impressive achievement and a real incentive to reach agreement on other issues.

Look for opportunities to act inconsistently with their perceptions. Perhaps the best way to change their perceptions is to send them a message different from what they expect. The visit of Egypt's President Sadat to Jerusalem in November 1977 provides an outstanding example of such an action. The Israelis saw Egypt and Sadat as their enemy, the man and country that launched a surprise attack on them four years before. To alter that perception, to help persuade the Israelis that he too desired peace, Sadat flew to the capital of his enemies, a disputed capital which not even the United States, Israel's best friend, had recognized. Instead of acting as an enemy, Sadat acted as a partner. Without this dramatic move, it is hard to imagine the signing of an Egyptian-Israeli peace treaty.

Give them a stake in the outcome by making sure they participate in the process. If they are not involved in the process, they are hardly likely to approve the product. It is that simple. If you go to the state insurance commissioner prepared for battle after a long investigation, it is not surprising that he is going to feel threatened and resist your conclusions. If you fail to ask an employee whether he wants an assignment with responsibility, don't be surprised to find out that he resents it. If you want the other side to accept a disagreeable conclusion, it is crucial that you involve them in the process of reaching that conclusion.

This is precisely what people tend not to do. When you have a difficult issue to handle, your instinct is to leave the hard part until last. "Let's be sure we have the whole thing worked out before we approach the Commissioner." The Commissioner, however, is much more likely to agree to a revision of the regulations if he feels that he has had a part in drafting it. This way the revision becomes just one more small step in the long drafting process that produced his original regulation rather than someone's attempt to butcher his completed product.

In South Africa, white moderates were trying at one point to abolish the discriminatory pass laws. How? By meeting in an all-white parliamentary committee to discuss proposals. Yet, however meritorious those proposals might prove, they would be insufficient, not necessarily because of their substance, but because they would be the product of a process in which no blacks were included. The blacks would hear, "We superior whites are going to figure out how to solve your problems." It would be the "white man's burden" all over again, which was the problem to start with.

Even if the terms of an agreement seem favorable, the other side may reject them simply out of a suspicion born of their exclusion from the drafting process. Agreement becomes much easier if both parties feel ownership of the ideas. The whole process of negotiation becomes stronger as each side puts their imprimatur bit by bit on a developing solution. Each criticism of the terms and consequent change, each concession, is a personal mark that the negotiator leaves on a proposal. A proposal evolves that bears enough of the suggestions of both sides for each to feel it is theirs.

To involve the other side, get them involved early. Ask

their advice. Giving credit generously for ideas wherever possible will give them a personal stake in defending those ideas to others. It may be hard to resist the temptation to take credit for yourself, but forbearance pays off handsomely. Apart from the substantive merits, the feeling of participation in the process is perhaps the single most important factor in determining whether a negotiator accepts a proposal. In a sense, the process *is* the product.

Face-saving: Make your proposals consistent with their values. In the English language, "face-saving" carries a derogatory flavor. People say, "We are doing that just to let them save face," implying that a little pretense has been created to allow someone to go along without feeling badly. The tone implies ridicule.

This is a grave misunderstanding of the role and importance of face-saving. Face-saving reflects a person's need to reconcile the stand he takes in a negotiation or an agreement with his principles and with his past words and deeds.

The judicial process concerns itself with the same subject. When a judge writes an opinion on a court ruling, he is saving face, not only for himself and for the judicial system, but for the parties. Instead of just telling one party, "You win," and telling the other, "You lose," he explains how his decision is consistent with principle, law, and precedent. He wants to appear not as arbitrary, but as behaving in a proper fashion. A negotiator is no different.

Often in a negotiation people will continue to hold out not because the proposal on the table is inherently unacceptable, but simply because they want to avoid the feeling or the appearance of backing down to the other side. If the substance can be phrased or conceptualized differently so that it seems a fair outcome, they will then accept it. Terms negotiated between a major city and its Hispanic community on municipal jobs were unacceptable to the mayor — until the agreement was withdrawn and the mayor was allowed to announce the same terms as his own decision, carrying out a campaign promise.

Face-saving involves reconciling an agreement with principle and with the self-image of the negotiators. Its importance should not be underestimated.

Emotion

In a negotiation, particularly in a bitter dispute, feelings may be more important than talk. The parties may be more ready for battle than for cooperatively working out a solution to a common problem. People often come to a negotiation realizing that the stakes are high and feeling threatened. Emotions on one side will generate emotions on the other. Fear may breed anger, and anger, fear. Emotions may quickly bring a negotiation to an impasse or an end.

First recognize and understand emotions, theirs and yours. Look at yourself during the negotiation. Are you feeling nervous? Is your stomach upset? Are you angry at the other side? Listen to them and get a sense of what their emotions are. You may find it useful to write down what you feel — perhaps fearful, worried, angry — and then how you might like to feel — confident, relaxed. Do the same for them.

In dealing with negotiators who represent their organizations, it is easy to treat them as mere mouthpieces without emotions. It is important to remember that they too, like you, have personal feelings, fears, hopes, and dreams. Their careers may be at stake. There may be issues on which they are particularly sensitive and others on which they are particularly proud. Nor are the problems of emotion limited to the negotiators. Constituents have emotions too. A constituent may have an even more simplistic and adversarial view of the situation.

Ask yourself what is producing the emotions. Why are you

angry? Why are they angry? Are they responding to past grievances and looking for revenge? Are emotions spilling over
from one issue to another? Are personal problems at home
interfering with business? In the Middle East negotiation, Israelis and Palestinians alike feel a threat to their existence as
peoples and have developed powerful emotions that now per-
meate even the most concrete practical issue, like distribution
of water in the West Bank, so that it becomes almost impossible to discuss and resolve. Because in the larger picture
both peoples feel that their own survival is at stake, they see
every other issue in terms of survival.

Make emotions explicit and acknowledge them as legitimate.
Talk with the people on the other side about their emotions.
Talk about your own. It does not hurt to say, "You know,
the people on our side feel we have been mistreated and are
very upset. We're afraid an agreement will not be kept even
if one is reached. Rational or not, that is our concern. Personally, I think we may be wrong in fearing this, but that's a
feeling others have. Do the people on your side feel the same
way?" Making your feelings or theirs an explicit focus of discussion will not only underscore the seriousness of the problem, it will also make the negotiations less reactive and more
"pro-active." Freed from the burden of unexpressed emotions,
people will become more likely to work on the problem.

Allow the other side to let off steam. Often, one effective
way to deal with people's anger, frustration, and other negative emotions is to help them release those feelings. People
obtain psychological release through the simple process of re-
counting their grievances. If you come home wanting to tell
your husband about everything that went wrong at the office,
you will become even more frustrated if he says, "Don't bother
telling me; I'm sure you had a hard day. Let's skip it." The
same is true for negotiators. Letting off steam may make it
easier to talk rationally later. Moreover, if a negotiator makes
an angry speech and thereby shows his constituency that he

is not being "soft," they may give him a freer hand in the negotiation. He can then rely on a reputation for toughness to protect him from criticism later if he eventually enters into an agreement.

Hence, instead of interrupting polemical speeches or walking out on the other party, you may decide to control yourself, sit there, and allow them to pour out their grievances at you. When constituents are listening, such occasions may release their frustration as well as the negotiator's. Perhaps the best strategy to adopt while the other side lets off steam is to listen quietly without responding to their attacks, and occasionally to ask the speaker to continue until he has spoken his last word. In this way, you offer little support to the inflammatory substance, give the speaker every encouragement to speak himself out, and leave little or no residue to fester.

Don't react to emotional outbursts. Releasing emotions can prove risky if it leads to an emotional reaction. If not controlled, it can result in a violent quarrel. One unusual and effective technique to contain the impact of emotions was used in the 1950s by the Human Relations Committee, a labor-management group set up in the steel industry to handle emerging conflicts before they became serious problems. The members of the committee adopted the rule that only one person could get angry at a time. This made it legitimate for others not to respond stormily to an angry outburst. It also made letting off emotional steam easier by making an outburst itself more legitimate: "That's OK. It's his turn." The rule has the further advantage of helping people control their emotions. Breaking the rule implies that you have lost self-control, so you lose some face.

Use symbolic gestures. Any lover knows that to end a quarrel the simple gesture of bringing a red rose goes a long way. Acts that would produce a constructive emotional impact on one side often involve little or no cost to the other. A note of sympathy, a statement of regret, a visit to a cemetery, delivering a small present for a grandchild, shaking hands or embracing, eating together — all may be priceless opportunities to improve a hostile emotional situation at small cost. On many occasions an apology can defuse emotions effectively, even when you do not acknowledge personal responsibility for the action or admit an intention to harm. An apology may be one of the least costly and most rewarding investments you can make.

Communication

Without communication there is no negotiation. Negotiation is a process of communicating back and forth for the purpose of reaching a joint decision. Communication is never an easy thing, even between people who have an enormous background of shared values and experience. Couples who have lived with each other for thirty years still have misunderstandings every day. It is not surprising, then, to find poor communication between people who do not know each other well and who may feel hostile and suspicious of one another. Whatever you say, you should expect that the other side will almost always hear something different.

There are three big problems in communication. First, negotiators may not be talking to each other, or at least not in such a way as to be understood. Frequently each side has given up on the other and is no longer attempting any serious communication with it. Instead they talk merely to impress third parties or their own constituency. Rather than trying to dance with their negotiating partner toward a mutually agreeable outcome, they try to trip him up. Rather than trying to talk their partner into a more constructive step, they try to talk the spectators into taking sides. Effective communication between the parties is all but impossible if each plays to the gallery.

Even if you are talking directly and clearly to them, they may not be hearing you. This constitutes the second problem in communication. Note how often people don't seem to pay enough attention to what you say. Probably equally often, you would be unable to repeat what they had said. In a negotiation, you may be so busy thinking about what you are going to say next, how you are going to respond to that last point or how you are going to frame your next argument, that you forget to listen to what the other side is saying now. Or you may be listening more attentively to your constituency than to the other side. Your constituents, after all, are the ones to whom you will have to account for the results of the negotiation. They are the ones you are trying to satisfy. It is not surprising that you should want to pay close attention to them. But if you are not hearing what the other side is saying, there is no communication.

The third communication problem is misunderstanding. What one says, the other may misinterpret. Even when negotiators are in the same room, communication from one to the other can seem like sending smoke signals in a high wind. Where the parties speak different languages the chance for misinterpretation is compounded. For example, in Persian, the word "compromise" apparently lacks the positive meaning it has in English of "a midway solution both sides can live with," but has only a negative meaning as in "her virtue was compromised" or "our integrity was compromised." Similarly, the word "mediator" in Persian suggests "meddler," someone who is barging in uninvited. In early 1980 U.N. Secretary General Waldheim flew to Iran to deal with the hostage question. His efforts were seriously set back when Iranian national radio and television broadcast in Persian a remark he reportedly made on his arrival in Tehran: "I have come as a *mediator* to work out a *compromise*." Within an hour of the broadcast, his car was being stoned by angry Iranians.

What can be done about these three problems of communication?

Listen actively and acknowledge what is being said. The need for listening is obvious, yet it is difficult to listen well, especially under the stress of an ongoing negotiation. Listening enables you to understand their perceptions, feel their emotions, and hear what they are trying to say. Active listening improves not only what you hear, but also what they say. If you pay attention and interrupt occasionally to say, "Did I understand correctly that you are saying that . . .?" the other side will realize that they are not just killing time, not just going through a routine. They will also feel the satisfaction of being heard and understood. It has been said that the cheapest concession you can make to the other side is to let them know they have been heard.

Standard techniques of good listening are to pay close attention to what is said, to ask the other party to spell out carefully and clearly exactly what they mean, and to request that ideas be repeated if there is any ambiguity or uncertainty. Make it your task while listening not to phrase a response, but to understand them as they see themselves. Take in their perceptions, their needs, and their constraints.

Many consider it a good tactic not to give the other side's case too much attention, and not to admit any legitimacy in their point of view. A good negotiator does just the reverse. Unless you acknowledge what they are saying and demonstrate that you understand them, they may believe you have not heard them. When you then try to explain a different point of view, they will suppose that you still have not grasped what they mean. They will say to themselves, "I told him my view, but now he's saying something different, so he must not have understood it." Then instead of listening to your point, they will be considering how to make their argument in a new way so that this time maybe you will fathom it. So show that you understand them. "Let me see whether I follow what you are telling me. From your point of view, the situation looks like this. . . ."

As you repeat what you understood them to have said, phrase it *positively* from their point of view, making the strength of their case clear. You might say, "You have a strong case. Let me see if I can explain it. Here's the way it strikes me. . . ." Understanding is not agreeing. One can at the same time understand perfectly and disagree completely with what the other side is saying. But unless you can convince them that you do grasp how they see it, you may be unable to explain your viewpoint to them. Once you have made their case for them, then come back with the problems you find in their proposal. If you can put their case better than they can, and then refute it, you maximize the chance of initiating a constructive dialogue on the merits and minimize the chance of their believing you have misunderstood them.

Speak to be understood. Talk to the other side. It is easy to forget sometimes that a negotiation is not a debate. Nor is it a trial. You are not trying to persuade some third party. The person you are trying to persuade is seated at the table with you. If a negotiation is to be compared with a legal proceeding, the situation resembles that of two judges trying to reach agreement on how to decide a case. Try putting yourself in that role, treating your opposite number as a fellow judge with whom you are attempting to work out a joint opinion. In this context it is clearly unpersuasive to blame the other party for the problem, to engage in name-calling, or to raise your voice. On the contrary, it will help to recognize explicitly that they see the situation differently and to try to go forward as people with a joint problem.

To reduce the dominating and distracting effect that the press, home audiences, and third parties may have, it is useful to establish private and confidential means of communicating with the other side. You can also improve communication by limiting the size of the group meeting. In the negotiations over the city of Trieste in 1954, for example, little progress was made in the talks among Yugoslavia, Britain, and the United States until the three principal negotiators abandoned their large delegations and started meeting alone and informally in a private house. A good case can be made for changing Woodrow Wilson's appealing slogan "Open covenants openly arrived at" to "Open covenants privately arrived at." No matter how many people are involved in a negotiation, important decisions are typically made when no more than two people are in the room.

Speak about yourself, not about them. In many negotiations, each side explains and condemns at great length the motivations and intentions of the other side. It is more persuasive, however, to describe a problem in terms of its impact on you than in terms of what they did or why: "I feel let down" instead of "You broke your word." "We feel discriminated against" rather than "You're a racist." If you make a statement about them that they believe is untrue, they will ignore you or get angry; they will not focus on your concern. But a statement about how you feel is difficult to challenge. You convey the same information without provoking a defensive reaction that will prevent them from taking it in.

Speak for a purpose. Sometimes the problem is not too little communication, but too much. When anger and misperception are high, some thoughts are best left unsaid. At other times, full disclosure of how flexible you are may make it harder to reach agreement rather than easier. If you let me know that you would be willing to sell a house for $40,000, after I have said that I would be willing to pay as much as $45,000, we may have more trouble striking a deal than if you had just kept quiet. The moral is: Before making a significant statement, know what you want to communicate or find out, and know what purpose this information will serve.

Prevention works best

The techniques just described for dealing with problems of
perception, emotion, and communication usually work well.
However, the best time for handling people problems is before
they become people problems. This means building a personal
and organizational relationship with the other side that can
cushion the people on each side against the knocks of negotiation. It also means structuring the negotiating game in ways
that separate the substantive problem from the relationship
and protect people's egos from getting involved in substantive
discussions.

Build a working relationship. Knowing the other side personally really does help. It is much easier to attribute dia-
bolical intentions to an unknown abstraction called the "other
side" than to someone you know personally. Dealing with a
classmate, a colleague, a friend, or even a friend of a friend
is quite different from dealing with a stranger. The more
quickly you can turn a stranger into someone you know, the
easier a negotiation is likely to become. You have less difficulty understanding where they are coming from. You have a
foundation of trust to build upon in a difficult negotiation.
You have smooth, familiar communication routines. It is easier
to defuse tension with a joke or an informal aside.

The time to develop such a relationship is before the negotiation begins. Get to know them and find out about their likes
and dislikes. Find ways to meet them informally. Try arriving
early to chat before the negotiation is scheduled to start, and
linger after it ends. Benjamin Franklin's favorite technique
was to ask an adversary if he could borrow a certain book.
This would flatter the person and give him the comfortable
feeling of knowing that Franklin owed him a favor.

Face the problem, not the people. If negotiators view themselves as adversaries in a personal face-to-face confrontation,
it is difficult to separate their relationship from the substantive
problem. In that context, anything one negotiator says about

the problem seems to be directed personally at the other and is received that way. Each side tends to become defensive and reactive and to ignore the other side's legitimate interests altogether.

A more effective way for the parties to think of themselves is as partners in a hardheaded, side-by-side search for a fair agreement advantageous to each.

Like two shipwrecked sailors in a lifeboat at sea quarreling over limited rations and supplies, negotiators may begin by seeing each other as adversaries. Each may view the other as a hindrance. To survive, however, those two sailors will want to disentangle the objective problems from the people. They will want to identify the needs of each, whether for shade, medicine, water, or food. They will want to go further and treat the meeting of those needs as a shared problem, along with other shared problems like keeping watch, catching rainwater, and getting the lifeboat to shore. Seeing themselves as engaged in side-by-side efforts to solve a mutual problem, the sailors will become better able to reconcile their conflicting interests as well as to advance their shared interests. Similarly with two negotiators. However difficult personal relations may be between us, you and I become better able to reach an amicable reconciliation of our various interests when we accept that task as a shared problem and face it jointly.

To help the other side change from a face-to-face orientation to side-by-side, you might raise the issue with them explicitly. "Look, we're both lawyers [diplomats, businessmen, family, etc.]. Unless we try to satisfy your interests, we are hardly likely to reach an agreement that satisfies mine, and vice versa. Let's look together at the problem of how to satisfy our collective interests." Alternatively, you could start treating the negotiation as a side-by-side process and by your actions make it desirable for them to join in.

It helps to sit literally on the same side of a table and to have in front of you the contract, the map, the blank pad of paper, or whatever else depicts the problem. If you have established a basis for mutual trust, so much the better. But however precarious your relationship may be, try to structure the negotiation as a side-by-side activity in which the two of you — with your differing interests and perceptions, and your emotional involvement — jointly face a common task.

Separating the people from the problem is not something you can do once and forget about; you have to keep working at it. The basic approach is to deal with the people as human beings and with the problem on its merits. How to do the latter is the subject of the next three chapters.

3 | Focus on Interests, Not Positions

Consider the story of two men quarreling in a library. One wants the window open and the other wants it closed. They bicker back and forth about how much to leave it open: a crack, halfway, three quarters of the way. No solution satisfies them both.

Enter the librarian. She asks one why he wants the window open: "To get some fresh air." She asks the other why he wants it closed: "To avoid the draft." After thinking a minute, she opens wide a window in the next room, bringing in fresh air without a draft.

For a wise solution reconcile interests, not positions

This story is typical of many negotiations. Since the parties' problem appears to be a conflict of positions, and since their goal is to agree on a position, they naturally tend to think and talk about positions — and in the process often reach an impasse.

The librarian could not have invented the solution she did if she had focused only on the two men's stated positions of wanting the window open or closed. Instead she looked to their underlying interests of fresh air and no draft. This difference between positions and interests is crucial.

Interests define the problem. The basic problem in a negotiation lies not in conflicting positions, but in the conflict between each side's needs, desires, concerns, and fears. The
parties may say:

"I am trying to get him to stop that real estate development next door."

Or "We disagree. He wants $50,000 for the house. I won't
pay a penny more than $47,500."

But on a more basic level the problem is:

"He needs the cash; I want peace and quiet."

Or "He needs at least $50,000 to settle with his ex-wife. I
told my family that I wouldn't pay more than $47,500 for a
house."

Such desires and concerns are *interests*. Interests motivate
people; they are the silent movers behind the hubbub of positions. Your position is something you have decided upon.
Your interests are what caused you to so decide.

The Egyptian-Israeli peace treaty blocked out at Camp
David in 1978 demonstrates the usefulness of looking behind
positions. Israel had occupied the Egyptian Sinai Peninsula
since the Six Day War of 1967. When Egypt and Israel sat
down together in 1978 to negotiate a peace, their positions
were incompatible. Israel insisted on keeping some of the
Sinai. Egypt, on the other hand, insisted that every inch of
the Sinai be returned to Egyptian sovereignty. Time and again,
people drew maps showing possible boundary lines that would
divide the Sinai between Egypt and Israel. Compromising in
this way was wholly unacceptable to Egypt. To go back to the
situation as it was in 1967 was equally unacceptable to Israel.

Looking to their interests instead of their positions made it
possible to develop a solution. Israel's interest lay in security;
they did not want Egyptian tanks poised on their border
ready to roll across at any time. Egypt's interest lay in sovereignty; the Sinai had been part of Egypt since the time of

the Pharaohs. After centuries of domination by Greeks, Romans, Turks, French, and British, Egypt had only recently regained full sovereignty and was not about to cede territory to another foreign conqueror.

At Camp David, President Sadat of Egypt and Prime Minister Begin of Israel agreed to a plan that would return the Sinai to complete Egyptian sovereignty and, by demilitarizing large areas, would still assure Israeli security. The Egyptian flag would fly everywhere, but Egyptian tanks would be nowhere near Israel.

Reconciling interests rather than positions works for two reasons. First, for every interest there usually exist several possible positions that could satisfy it. All too often people simply adopt the most obvious position, as Israel did, for example, in announcing that they intended to keep part of the Sinai. When you do look behind opposed positions for the motivating interests, you can often find an alternative position which meets not only your interests but theirs as well. In the Sinai, demilitarization was one such alternative.

Reconciling interests rather than compromising between positions also works because behind opposed positions lie many more interests than conflicting ones.

Behind opposed positions lie shared and compatible interests, as well as conflicting ones. We tend to assume that because the other side's positions are opposed to ours, their interests must also be opposed. If we have an interest in defending ourselves, then they must want to attack us. If we have an interest in minimizing the rent, then their interest must be to maximize it. In many negotiations, however, a close examination of the underlying interests will reveal the existence of many more interests that are shared or compatible than ones that are opposed.

For example, look at the interests a tenant shares with a prospective landlord:

1. Both want stability. The landlord wants a stable tenant; the tenant wants a permanent address.

2. Both would like to see the apartment well maintained. The tenant is going to live there; the landlord wants to increase the value of the apartment as well as the reputation of the building.

3. Both are interested in a good relationship with each other. The landlord wants a tenant who pays the rent regularly; the tenant wants a responsive landlord who will carry out the necessary repairs.

They may have interests that do not conflict but simply differ. For example:

1. The tenant may not want to deal with fresh paint, to which he is allergic. The landlord will not want to pay the costs of repainting all the other apartments.

2. The landlord would like the security of a down payment of the first month's rent, and he may want it by tomorrow. The tenant, knowing that this is a good apartment, may be indifferent on the question of paying tomorrow or later.

When weighed against these shared and divergent interests, the opposed interests in minimizing the rent and maximizing the return seem more manageable. The shared interests will likely result in a long lease, an agreement to share the cost of improving the apartment, and efforts by both parties to accommodate each other in the interest of a good relationship. The divergent interests may perhaps be reconciled by a down payment tomorrow and an agreement by the landlord to paint the apartment provided the tenant buys the paint. The precise amount of the rent is all that remains to be settled, and the market for rental apartments may define that fairly well.

Agreement is often made possible precisely because interests differ. You and a shoe-seller may both like money and shoes. Relatively, his interest in the thirty dollars exceeds his interest in the shoes. For you, the situation is reversed: you like the shoes better than the thirty dollars. Hence the deal. Shared interests and differing but complementary interests can both serve as the building blocks for a wise agreement.

How do you identify interests?

The benefit of looking behind positions for interests is clear. How to go about it is less clear. A position is likely to be concrete and explicit; the interests underlying it may well be unexpressed, intangible, and perhaps inconsistent. How do you go about understanding the interests involved in a negotiation, remembering that figuring out *their* interests will be at least as important as figuring out *yours*?

Ask "Why?" One basic technique is to put yourself in their shoes. Examine each position they take, and ask yourself "Why?" Why, for instance, does your landlord prefer to fix the rent — in a five-year lease — year by year? The answer you may come up with, to be protected against increasing costs, is probably one of his interests. You can also ask the landlord himself why he takes a particular position. If you do, make clear that you are asking not for justification of this position, but for an understanding of the needs, hopes, fears, or desires that it serves. "What's your basic concern, Mr. Jones, in wanting the lease to run for no more than three years?"

Ask "Why not?" Think about their choice. One of the most useful ways to uncover interests is first to identify the basic decision that those on the other side probably see you asking them for, and then to ask yourself why they have not made that decision. What interests of theirs stand in the way? If you are trying to change their minds, the starting point is to figure out where their minds are now.

Consider, for example, the negotiations between the United

States and Iran in 1980 over the release of the fifty-two U.S. diplomats and embassy personnel held hostage in Tehran by student militants. While there were a host of serious obstacles to a resolution of this dispute, the problem is illuminated simply by looking at the choice of a typical student leader. The demand of the United States was clear: "Release the hostages." During much of 1980 each student leader's choice must have looked something like that illustrated by the balance sheet below.

AS OF: Spring 1980

Presently Perceived Choice of: An Iranian student leader
Question Faced: "Shall I press for immediate release of the American hostages?"

IF I SAY YES	IF I SAY NO
— I sell out the Revolution.	+ I uphold the Revolution.
— I will be criticized as pro-American.	+ I will be praised for defending Islam.
— The others will probably not agree with me; if they do and we release the hostages, then:	+ We will probably all stick together.
	+ We get fantastic TV coverage to tell the world about our grievances.
— Iran looks weak.	+ Iran looks strong.
— We back down to the U.S.	+ We stand up to the U.S.
— We get nothing (no Shah, no money).	+ We have a chance of getting something (at least our money back).
— We do not know what the U.S. will do.	+ The hostages provide some protection against U.S. intervention.

BUT:

+ There is a chance that economic sanctions might end.

+ Our relations with other nations, especially in Europe, may improve.

BUT:

— Economic sanctions will no doubt continue.

— Our relations with other nations, especially in Europe, will suffer.

— Inflation and economic problems will continue.

— There is a risk that the U.S. might take military action (but a martyr's death is the most glorious).

HOWEVER:

+ The U.S. may make further commitments about our money, nonintervention, ending sanctions, etc.

+ We can always release the hostages later.

If a typical student leader's choice did look even approximately like this, it is understandable why the militant students held the hostages so long: As outrageous and illegal as the original seizure was, once the hostages had been seized it was not irrational for the students to *keep* holding them from one day to the next, waiting for a more promising time to release them.

In constructing the other side's presently perceived choice the first question to ask is "Whose decision do I want to affect?" The second question is what decision people on the other side now see you asking them to make. If *you* have no idea what they think they are being called on to do, *they* may not either. That alone may explain why they are not deciding as you would like.

Now analyze the consequences, as the other side would probably see them, of agreeing or refusing to make the decision you are asking for. You may find a checklist of consequences such as the following helpful in this task:

Impact on my interests
- Will I lose or gain political support?
- Will colleagues criticize or praise me?

Impact on the group's interests
- What will be the short-term consequences? The long-term consequences?
- What will be the economic consequences (political, legal, psychological, military, etc.)?
- What will be the effect on outside supporters and public opinion?
- Will the precedent be good or bad?
- Will making this decision prevent doing something better?
- Is the action consistent with our principles? Is it "right"?
- Can I do it later if I want?

In this entire process it would be a mistake to try for great precision. Only rarely will you deal with a decision-maker who writes down and weighs the pros and cons. You are trying to understand a very human choice, not making a mathematical calculation.

Realize that each side has multiple interests. In almost every negotiation each side will have many interests, not just one. As a tenant negotiating a lease, for example, you may want to obtain a favorable rental agreement, to reach it quickly with little effort, and to maintain a good working relationship with your landlord. You will have not only a strong interest in *affecting* any agreement you reach, but also one in *effecting* an agreement. You will be simultaneously pursuing both your independent and your shared interests.

A common error in diagnosing a negotiating situation is to

assume that each person on the other side has the same interests. This is almost never the case. During the Vietnam war, President Johnson was in the habit of lumping together all the different members of the government of North Vietnam, the Vietcong in the south, and their Soviet and Chinese advisers and calling them collectively "he." "The enemy has to learn that *he* can't cross the United States with impunity. *He* is going to have to learn that aggression doesn't pay." It will be difficult to influence any such "him" (or even "them") to agree to anything if you fail to appreciate the differing interests of the various people and factions involved.

Thinking of negotiation as a two-person, two-sided affair can be illuminating, but it should not blind you to the usual presence of other persons, other sides, and other influences. In one baseball salary negotiation the general manager kept insisting that $200,000 was simply too much for a particular player, although other teams were paying at least that much to similarly talented players. In fact the manager felt his position was unjustifiable, but he had strict instructions from the club's owners to hold firm without explaining why, because they were in financial difficulties that they did not want the public to hear about.

Whether it is his employer, his client, his employees, his colleagues, his family, or his wife, every negotiator has a constituency to whose interests he is sensitive. To understand that negotiator's interests means to understand the variety of somewhat differing interests that he needs to take into account.

The most powerful interests are basic human needs. In searching for the basic interests behind a declared position, look particularly for those bedrock concerns which motivate all people. If you can take care of such basic needs, you increase the chance both of reaching agreement and, if an agreement is reached, of the other side's keeping to it. Basic human needs include:

- security
- economic well-being
- a sense of belonging
- recognition
- control over one's life

As fundamental as they are, basic human needs are easy to overlook. In many negotiations, we tend to think that the only interest involved is money. Yet even in a negotiation over a monetary figure, such as the amount of alimony to be specified in a separation agreement, much more can be involved. What does a wife really want in asking for $500 a week in alimony? Certainly she is interested in her economic well-being, but what else? Possibly she wants the money in order to feel psychologically secure. She may also want it for recognition: to feel that she is treated fairly and as an equal. Perhaps the husband can ill afford to pay $500 a week, and perhaps his wife does not need that much, yet she will likely accept less only if her needs for security and recognition are met in other ways.

What is true for individuals remains equally true for groups and nations. Negotiations are not likely to make much progress as long as one side believes that the fulfillment of their basic human needs is being threatened by the other. In negotiations between the United States and Mexico, the U.S. wanted a low price for Mexican natural gas. Assuming that this was a negotiation over money, the U.S. Secretary of Energy refused to approve a price increase negotiated with the Mexicans by a U.S. oil consortium. Since the Mexicans had no other potential buyer at the time, he assumed that they would then lower their asking price. But the Mexicans had a strong interest not only in getting a good price for their gas but also in being treated with respect and a sense of equality. The U.S. action seemed like one more attempt to bully Mexico; it produced enormous anger. Rather than sell their gas, the Mexican government began to burn it off, and any chance of agreement on a lower price became politically impossible.

To take another example, in the negotiations over the future of Northern Ireland, Protestant leaders tend to ignore the Catholics' need for both belonging and recognition, for being accepted and treated as equals. In turn, Catholic leaders often appear to give too little weight to the Protestants' need to feel secure. Treating Protestant fears as "their problem" rather than as a legitimate concern needing attention makes it even more difficult to negotiate a solution.

Make a list. To sort out the various interests of each side, it helps to write them down as they occur to you. This will not only help you remember them; it will also enable you to improve the quality of your assessment as you learn new information and to place interests in their estimated order of importance. Furthermore, it may stimulate ideas for how to meet these interests.

Talking about interests

The purpose of negotiating is to serve your interests. The chance of that happening increases when you communicate them. The other side may not know what your interests are, and you may not know theirs. One or both of you may be focusing on past grievances instead of on future concerns. Or you may not even be listening to each other. How do you discuss interests constructively without getting locked into rigid positions?

If you want the other side to take your interests into account, explain to them what those interests are. A member of a concerned citizens' group complaining about a construction project in the neighborhood should talk explicitly about such issues as ensuring children's safety and getting a good night's sleep. An author who wants to be able to give a great many of his books away should discuss the matter with his publisher.

The publisher has a shared interest in promotion and may be willing to offer the author a low price.

Make your interests come alive. If you go with a raging ulcer to see a doctor, you should not hope for much relief if you describe it as a mild stomachache. It is your job to have the other side understand exactly how important and legitimate your interests are.

One guideline is *be specific*. Concrete details not only make your description credible, they add impact. For example: "Three times in the last week, a child was almost run over by one of your trucks. About eight-thirty Tuesday morning that huge red gravel truck of yours, going north at almost forty miles an hour, had to swerve and barely missed hitting seven-year-old Loretta Johnson."

As long as you do not seem to imply that the other side's interests are unimportant or illegitimate, you can afford to take a strong stance in setting forth the seriousness of your concerns. Inviting the other side to "correct me if I'm wrong" shows your openness, and if they do not correct you, it implies that they accept your description of the situation.

Part of the task of impressing the other side with your interests lies in establishing the legitimacy of those interests. You want them to feel not that you are attacking them personally, but rather that the problem you face legitimately demands attention. You need to convince them that they might well feel the same way if they were in your shoes. "Do you have children? How would you feel if trucks were hurtling at forty miles per hour down the street where you live?"

Acknowledge their interests as part of the problem. Each of us tends to be so concerned with his or her own interests that we pay too little heed to the interests of others.

People listen better if they feel that you have understood them. They tend to think that those who understand them are intelligent and sympathetic people whose own opinions may be worth listening to. So if you want the other side to appreciate *your* interests, begin by demonstrating that you appreciate *theirs.*

"As I understand it, your interests as a construction company are basically to get the job done quickly at minimum cost and to preserve your reputation for safety and responsibility in the city. Have I understood you correctly? Do you have other important interests?"

In addition to demonstrating that you have understood their interests, it helps to acknowledge that their interests are part of the overall problem you are trying to solve. This is especially easy to do if you have shared interests: "It would be terrible for all of us if one of your trucks hit a child."

Put the problem before your answer. In talking to someone who represents a construction company, you might say, "We believe you should build a fence around the project within forty-eight hours and beginning immediately should restrict the speed of your trucks on Oak Street to fifteen miles an hour. Now let me tell you why. . . ." If you do, you can be quite certain that he will not be listening to the reasons. He has heard your position and is no doubt busy preparing arguments against it. He was probably disturbed by your tone or by the suggestion itself. As a result, your justification will slip by him altogether.

If you want someone to listen and understand your reasoning, give your interests and reasoning first and your conclusions or proposals later. Tell the company first about the dangers they are creating for young children and about your sleepless nights. Then they will be listening carefully, if only to try to figure out where you will end up on this question. And when you tell them, they will understand why.

Look forward, not back. It is surprising how often we simply react to what someone else has said or done. Two people will often fall into a pattern of discourse that resembles a negotiation, but really has no such purpose whatsoever. They disagree with each other over some issue, and the talk goes back and forth as though they were seeking agreement. In fact, the argument is being carried on as a ritual, or simply a pastime. Each is engaged in scoring points against the other or in gathering evidence to confirm views about the other that have long been held and are not about to be changed. Neither party is seeking agreement or is even trying to influence the other.

If you ask two people why they are arguing, the answer will typically identify a cause, not a purpose. Caught up in a quarrel, whether between husband and wife, between company and union, or between two businesses, people are more likely to respond to what the other side has said or done than to act in pursuit of their own long-term interests. "They can't treat me like that. If they think they're going to get away with that, they will have to think again. I'll show them."

The question "Why?" has two quite different meanings. One looks backward for a cause and treats our behavior as determined by prior events. The other looks forward for a purpose and treats our behavior as subject to our free will. We need not enter into a philosophical debate between free will and determinism in order to decide how to act. Either we have free will or it is determined that we behave as if we do. In either case, we make choices. We can *choose* to look back or to look forward.

You will satisfy your interests better if you talk about where you would like to go rather than about where you have come from. Instead of arguing with the other side about the past — about last quarter's costs (which were too high), last week's action (taken without adequate authority), or yesterday's performance (which was less than expected) — talk about what you want to have happen in the future. Instead of asking them to justify what they did yesterday, ask, "Who should do what tomorrow?"

Be concrete but flexible. In a negotiation you want to know where you are going and yet be open to fresh ideas. To avoid having to make a difficult decision on what to settle for,

people will often go into a negotiation with no other plan than
to sit down with the other side and see what they offer or
demand.

How can you move from identifying interests to developing
specific options and still remain flexible with regard to those
options? To convert your interests into concrete options, ask
yourself, "If tomorrow the other side agrees to go along with
me, what do I now think I would like them to go along
with?" To keep your flexibility, treat each option you formulate as simply illustrative. Think in terms of more than one
option that meets your interests. "Illustrative specificity" is
the key concept.

Much of what positional bargainers hope to achieve with
an opening position can be accomplished equally well with an
illustrative suggestion that generously takes care of your interest. For example, in a baseball contract negotiation, an
agent might say that "$250,000 a year would be the kind of
figure that should satisfy Cortez's interest in receiving the salary he feels he is worth. Something on the order of a five-year
contract should meet his need for job security."

Having thought about your interests, you should go into a
meeting not only with one or more specific options that would
meet your legitimate interests but also with an open mind. An
open mind is not an empty one.

Be hard on the problem, soft on the people. You can be
just as hard in talking about your interests as any negotiator
can be in talking about his position. In fact, it is usually ad-
visable to be hard. It may not be wise to commit yourself to
your position, but it is wise to commit yourself to your interests. This is the place in a negotiation to spend your aggres-
sive energies. The other side, being concerned with their own
interests, will tend to have overly optimistic expectations of
the range of possible agreements. Often the wisest solutions,
those that produce the maximum gain for you at the minimum
cost to the other side, are produced only by strongly advocat-

ing your interests. Two negotiators, each pushing hard for
their interests, will often stimulate each other's creativity in
thinking up mutually advantageous solutions.

The construction company, concerned with inflation, may
place a high value on its interest in keeping costs down and
in getting the job done on time. You may have to shake them
up. Some honest emotion may help restore a better balance
between profits and children's lives. Do not let your desire
to be conciliatory stop you from doing justice to your problem.
"Surely you're not saying that my son's life is worth less than
the price of a fence. You wouldn't say that about your son. I
don't believe you're an insensitive person, Mr. Jenkins. Let's
figure out how to solve this problem."

If they feel personally threatened by an attack on the problem, they may grow defensive and may cease to listen. This
is why it is important to separate the people from the problem. Attack the problem without blaming the people. Go even
further and be personally supportive: Listen to them with respect, show them courtesy, express your appreciation for their
time and effort, emphasize your concern with meeting their
basic needs, and so on. Show them that you are attacking the
problem, not them.

One useful rule of thumb is to give positive support to the
human beings on the other side equal in strength to the vigor
with which you emphasize the problem. This combination of
support and attack may seem inconsistent. Psychologically, it
is; the inconsistency helps make it work. A well-known theory
of psychology, the theory of cognitive dissonance, holds that
people dislike inconsistency and will act to eliminate it. By
attacking a problem, such as speeding trucks on a neighborhood street, and at the same time giving the company representative positive support, you create cognitive dissonance for
him. To overcome this dissonance, he will be tempted to dis-
sociate himself from the problem in order to join you in doing
something about it.

Fighting hard on the substantive issues increases the pressure for an effective solution; giving support to the human beings on the other side tends to improve your relationship and to increase the likelihood of reaching agreement. It is the combination of support and attack which works; either alone is likely to be insufficient.

Negotiating hard for your interests does not mean being closed to the other side's point of view. Quite the contrary. You can hardly expect the other side to listen to your interests and discuss the options you suggest if you don't take their interests into account and show yourself to be open to their suggestions. Successful negotiation requires being both firm *and* open.

4 | Invent Options for Mutual Gain

The case of Israel and Egypt negotiating over who should keep how much of the Sinai Peninsula illustrates both a major problem in negotiation and a key opportunity.

The problem is a common one. There seems to be no way to split the pie that leaves both parties satisfied. Often you are negotiating along a single dimension, such as the amount of territory, the price of a car, the length of a lease on an apartment, or the size of a commission on a sale. At other times you face what appears to be an either/or choice that is either markedly favorable to you or to the other side. In a divorce settlement, who gets the house? Who gets custody of the children? You may see the choice as one between winning and losing — and neither side will agree to lose. Even if you do win and get the car for $5,000, the lease for five years, or the house and kids, you have a sinking feeling that they will not let you forget it. Whatever the situation, your choices seem limited.

The Sinai example also makes clear the opportunity. A creative option like a demilitarized Sinai can often make the difference between deadlock and agreement. One lawyer we know attributes his success directly to his ability to invent solutions advantageous to both his client and the other side. He expands the pie before dividing it. Skill at inventing options is one of the most useful assets a negotiator can have.

Yet all too often negotiators end up like the proverbial sisters who quarreled over an orange. After they finally agreed to divide the orange in half, the first sister took her half, ate the fruit, and threw away the peel, while the other threw away the fruit and used the peel from her half in baking a cake. All too often negotiators "leave money on the table" — they fail to reach agreement when they might have, or the agreement they do reach could have been better for each side. Too many negotiations end up with half an orange for each side instead of the whole fruit for one and the whole peel for the other. Why?

DIAGNOSIS

As valuable as it is to have many options, people involved in a negotiation rarely sense a need for them. In a dispute, people usually believe that they know the right answer — their view should prevail. In a contract negotiation they are equally likely to believe that their offer is reasonable and should be adopted, perhaps with some adjustment in the price. All available answers appear to lie along a straight line between their position and yours. Often the only creative thinking shown is to suggest splitting the difference.

In most negotiations there are four major obstacles that inhibit the inventing of an abundance of options: (1) premature judgment; (2) searching for the single answer; (3) the assumption of a fixed pie; and (4) thinking that "solving their problem is their problem." In order to overcome these constraints, you need to understand them.

Premature judgment

Inventing options does not come naturally. *Not* inventing is the normal state of affairs, even when you are outside a stressful negotiation. If you were asked to name the one person in the world most deserving of the Nobel Peace Prize, any answer you might start to propose would immediately encounter your reservations and doubts. How could you be sure that that person was the *most* deserving? Your mind might well go blank, or you might throw out a few answers that would reflect conventional thinking: "Well, maybe the Pope, or the President."

Nothing is so harmful to inventing as a critical sense waiting to pounce on the drawbacks of any new idea. Judgment hinders imagination.

Under the pressure of a forthcoming negotiation, your critical sense is likely to be sharper. Practical negotiation appears to call for practical thinking, not wild ideas.

Your creativity may be even more stifled by the presence of those on the other side. Suppose you are negotiating with your boss over your salary for the coming year. You have asked for a $4,000 raise; your boss has offered you $1,500, a figure that you have indicated is unsatisfactory. In a tense situation like this you are not likely to start inventing imaginative solutions. You may fear that if you suggest some bright half-baked idea like taking half the increase in a raise and half in additional benefits, you might look foolish. Your boss might say, "Be serious. You know better than that. It would upset company policy. I am surprised that you even suggested it." If on the spur of the moment you invent a possible option of spreading out the raise over time, he may take it as an offer: "I'm prepared to start negotiating on that basis." Since he may take whatever you say as a commitment, you will think twice before saying anything.

You may also fear that by inventing options you will disclose some piece of information that will jeopardize your bargaining position. If you should suggest, for example, that the company help finance the house you are about to buy, your boss may conclude that you intend to stay and that you will in the end accept any raise in salary he is prepared to offer.

Searching for the single answer

In most people's minds, inventing simply is not part of the negotiating process. People see their job as narrowing the gap between positions, not broadening the options available. They tend to think, "We're having a hard enough time agreeing as it is. The last thing we need is a bunch of different ideas." Since the end product of negotiation is a single decision, they fear that free-floating discussion will only delay and confuse the process.

If the first impediment to creative thinking is premature criticism, the second is premature closure. By looking from the outset for the single best answer, you are likely to short-circuit a wiser decision-making process in which you select from a large number of possible answers.

The assumption of a fixed pie

A third explanation for why there may be so few good options on the table is that each side sees the situation as essentially either/or — either I get what is in dispute or you do. A negotiation often appears to be a "fixed-sum" game; $100 more for you on the price of a car means $100 less for me. Why bother to invent if all the options are obvious and I can satisfy you only at my own expense?

Thinking that "solving their problem is their problem"

A final obstacle to inventing realistic options lies in each side's concern with only its own immediate interests. For a negotiator to reach an agreement that meets his own self-interest he needs to develop a solution which also appeals to the self-interest of the other. Yet emotional involvement on one side of an issue makes it difficult to achieve the detachment necessary to think up wise ways of meeting the interests

of both sides: "We've got enough problems of our own; they
can look after theirs." There also frequently exists a psychological reluctance to accord any legitimacy to the views of the
other side; it seems disloyal to think up ways to satisfy them.
Shortsighted self-concern thus leads a negotiator to develop
only partisan positions, partisan arguments, and one-sided
solutions.

PRESCRIPTION

To invent creative options, then, you will need (1) to separate the act of inventing options from the act of judging them;
(2) to broaden the options on the table rather than look for
a single answer; (3) to search for mutual gains; and (4) to
invent ways of making their decisions easy. Each of these
steps is discussed below.

Separate inventing from deciding

Since judgment hinders imagination, separate the creative act
from the critical one; separate the process of thinking up
possible decisions from the process of selecting among them.
Invent first, decide later.

As a negotiator, you will of necessity do much inventing
by yourself. It is not easy. By definition, inventing new ideas
requires you to think about things that are not already in
your mind. You should therefore consider the desirability of
arranging an inventing or brainstorming session with a few
colleagues or friends. Such a session can effectively separate
inventing from deciding.

A brainstorming session is designed to produce as many
ideas as possible to solve the problem at hand. The key ground
rule is to postpone all criticism and evaluation of ideas. The
group simply invents ideas without pausing to consider whether

they are good or bad, realistic or unrealistic. With those in-
hibitions removed, one idea should stimulate another, like
firecrackers setting off one another.

In a brainstorming session, people need not fear looking
foolish since wild ideas are explicitly encouraged. And in the
absence of the other side, negotiators need not worry about
disclosing confidential information or having an idea taken
as a serious commitment.

There is no one right way to run a brainstorming session.
Rather, you should tailor it to your needs and resources. In
doing so, you may find it useful to consider the following
guidelines.

Before brainstorming:

1. *Define your purpose.* Think of what you would like to
walk out of the meeting with.

2. *Choose a few participants.* The group should normally
be large enough to provide a stimulating interchange, yet
small enough to encourage both individual participation and
free-wheeling inventing — usually between five and eight
people.

3. *Change the environment.* Select a time and place distin-
guishing the session as much as possible from regular discussions. The more different a brainstorming session seems from
a normal meeting, the easier it is for participants to suspend
judgment.

4. *Design an informal atmosphere.* What does it take for
you and others to relax? It may be talking over a drink, or
meeting at a vacation lodge in some picturesque spot, or
simply taking off your tie and jacket during the meeting and
calling each other by your first names.

5. *Choose a facilitator.* Someone at the meeting needs to
facilitate — to keep the meeting on track, to make sure everyone gets a chance to speak, to enforce any ground rules, and
to stimulate discussion by asking questions.

During brainstorming:

1. *Seat the participants side by side facing the problem.*
The physical reinforces the psychological. Physically sitting
side by side can reinforce the mental attitude of tackling a
common problem together. People facing each other tend to
respond personally and engage in dialogue or argument; people sitting side by side in a semicircle of chairs facing a blackboard tend to respond to the problem depicted there.

2. *Clarify the ground rules, including the no-criticism rule.*
If the participants do not all know each other, the meeting
begins with introductions all around, followed by clarification
of the ground rules. Outlaw negative criticism of any kind.

Joint inventing produces new ideas because each of us invents only within the limits set by our working assumptions.
If ideas are shot down unless they appeal to all participants, the
implicit goal becomes to advance an idea that no one will shoot
down. If, on the other hand, wild ideas are encouraged, even
those that in fact lie well outside the realm of the possible, the
group may generate from these ideas other options that *are*
possible and that no one would previously have considered.

Other ground rules you may want to adopt are to make the
entire session off the record and to refrain from attributing
ideas to any participant.

3. *Brainstorm.* Once the purpose of the meeting is clear,
let your imaginations go. Try to come up with a long list of
ideas, approaching the question from every conceivable angle.

4. *Record the ideas in full view.* Recording ideas either on
a blackboard or, better, on large sheets of newsprint gives
the group a tangible sense of collective achievement; it reinforces the no-criticism rule; it reduces the tendency to repeat;
and it helps stimulate other ideas.

After brainstorming:

1. *Star the most promising ideas.* After brainstorming, relax the no-criticism rule in order to winnow out the most
promising ideas. You are still not at the stage of deciding;

you are merely nominating ideas worth developing further. Mark those ideas that members of the group think are best.

2. *Invent improvements for promising ideas.* Take one promising idea and invent ways to make it better and more realistic, as well as ways to carry it out. The task at this stage is to make the idea as attractive as you can. Preface constructive criticism with: "What I like best about that idea is . . . . Might it be better if . . . ?"

3. *Set up a time to evaluate ideas and decide.* Before you break up, draw up a selective and improved list of ideas from the session and set up a time for deciding which of these ideas to advance in your negotiation and how.

Consider brainstorming with the other side. Although more difficult than brainstorming with your own side, brainstorming with people from the other side can also prove extremely valuable. It is more difficult because of the increased risk that you will say something that prejudices your interests despite the rules established for a brainstorming session. You may disclose confidential information inadvertently or lead the other side to mistake an option you devise for an offer. Nevertheless, joint brainstorming sessions have the great advantages of producing ideas which take into account the interests of all those involved, of creating a climate of joint problem-solving, and of educating each side about the concerns of the other.

To protect yourself when brainstorming with the other side, distinguish the brainstorming session explicitly from a negotiating session where people state official views and speak on the record. People are so accustomed to meeting for the purpose of reaching agreement that any other purpose needs to be clearly stated.

To reduce the risk of appearing committed to any given idea, you can make a habit of advancing at least two alternatives at the same time. You can also put on the table options with which you obviously disagree. "I could give you the house for nothing, or you could pay me a million dollars in cash for

it, or . . . ." Since you are plainly not proposing either of these
ideas, the ones which follow are labeled as mere possibilities,
not proposals.

To get the flavor of a joint brainstorming session, let us
suppose the leaders of a local union are meeting with the management of a coal mine to brainstorm on ways to reduce unauthorized one- or two-day strikes. Ten people — five from
each side — are present, sitting around a table facing a blackboard. A neutral facilitator asks the participants for their ideas,
and writes them down on the blackboard.

FACILITATOR: OK, now let's see what ideas you have for dealing with this problem of unauthorized work stoppages. Let's try
to get ten ideas on the blackboard in five minutes. OK, let's start.
Tom?

TOM (UNION): Foremen ought to be able to settle a union member's grievance on the spot.

FACILITATOR: Good, I've got it down. Jim, you've got your
hand up.

JIM (MANAGEMENT): A union member ought to talk to his
foreman about a problem before taking any action that ——

TOM (UNION): They do, but the foremen don't listen.

FACILITATOR: Tom, please, no criticizing yet. We agreed to
postpone that until later, OK? How about you, Jerry? You look
like you've got an idea.

JERRY (UNION): When a strike issue comes up, the union members should be allowed to meet in the bathhouse immediately.

ROGER (MANAGEMENT): Management could agree to let the
bathhouse be used for union meetings and could assure the employees' privacy by shutting the doors and keeping the foremen out.

CAROL (MANAGEMENT): How about adopting the rule that there
will be no strike without giving the union leaders and management
a chance to work it out on the spot?

JERRY (UNION): How about speeding up the grievance procedure and having a meeting within twenty-four hours if the foreman and union member don't settle it between themselves?

KAREN (UNION): Yeah. And how about organizing some joint training for the union members and the foremen on how to handle their problems together?

PHIL (UNION): If a person does a good job, let him know it.

JOHN (MANAGEMENT): Establish friendly relations between union people and management people.

FACILITATOR: That sounds promising, John, but could you be more specific?

JOHN (MANAGEMENT): Well, how about organizing a union-management softball team?

TOM (UNION): And a bowling team too.

ROGER (MANAGEMENT): How about an annual picnic get-together for all the families?

And on it goes, as the participants brainstorm lots of ideas. Many of the ideas might never have come up except in such a brainstorming session, and some of them may prove effective in reducing unauthorized strikes. Time spent brainstorming together is surely among the best-spent time in negotiation.

But whether you brainstorm together or not, separating the act of developing options from the act of deciding on them is extremely useful in any negotiation. Discussing options differs radically from taking positions. Whereas one side's position will conflict with another's, options invite other options. The very language you use differs. It consists of questions, not assertions; it is open, not closed: "One option is . . . . What other options have you thought of?" "What if we agreed to this?" "How about doing it this way?" "How would this work?" "What would be wrong with that?" Invent before you decide.

Broaden your options

Even with the best of intentions, participants in a brainstorming session are likely to operate on the assumption that they are really looking for the *one* best answer, trying to find a needle in a haystack by picking up every blade of hay.

At this stage in a negotiation, however, you should not be looking for the right path. You are developing room within which to negotiate. Room can be made only by having a substantial number of markedly different ideas — ideas on which you and the other side can build later in the negotiation, and among which you can then jointly choose.

A vintner making a fine wine chooses his grapes from a number of varieties. A baseball team looking for star players will send talent scouts to scour the local leagues and college teams all over the nation. The same principle applies to negotiation. The key to wise decision-making, whether in wine-making, baseball, or negotiation, lies in selecting from a great number and variety of options.

If you were asked who should receive the Nobel Peace Prize this year, you would do well to answer "Well, let's think about it" and generate a list of about a hundred names from diplomacy, business, journalism, religion, law, agriculture, politics, academia, medicine, and other fields, making sure to dream up a lot of wild ideas. You would almost certainly end up with a better decision this way than if you tried to decide right from the start.

A brainstorming session frees people to think creatively. Once freed, they need ways to think about their problems and to generate constructive solutions.

Multiply options by shuttling between the specific and the general: The Circle Chart. The task of inventing options involves four types of thinking. One is thinking about a particular problem — the factual situation you dislike, for example, a smelly, polluted river that runs by your land. The second type of thinking is descriptive analysis — you diagnose an existing situation in general terms. You sort problems into categories and tentatively suggest causes. The river water may have a high content of various chemicals, or too little oxygen. You may suspect various upstream industrial plants. The third type of thinking, again in general terms, is to consider what ought, perhaps, to be done. Given the diagnoses you have made, you look for prescriptions that theory may suggest, such as reducing chemical effluent, reducing diversions of water, or bringing fresh water from some other river. The fourth and final type of thinking is to come up with some specific and feasible suggestions for action. Who might do what tomorrow to put one of these general approaches into practice? For instance, the state environmental agency might order an upstream industry to limit the quantity of chemical discharge.

The Circle Chart on the next page illustrates these four types of thinking and suggests them as steps to be taken in sequence. If all goes well, the specific action invented in this way will, if adopted, deal with your original problem.

The Circle Chart provides an easy way of using one good idea to generate others. With one useful action idea before you, you (or a group of you who are brainstorming) can go back and try to identify the general approach of which the action idea is merely one application. You can then think up other action ideas that would apply the same general approach to the real world. Similarly, you can go back one step further and ask, "If this theoretical approach appears useful, what is the diagnosis behind it?" Having articulated a diagnosis, you can generate other approaches for dealing with a problem analyzed in that way, and then look for actions putting these new approaches into practice. One good option on the table thus opens the door to asking about the theory that makes this option good and then using that theory to invent more options.

An example may illustrate the process. In dealing with the conflict over Northern Ireland, one idea might be to have

CIRCLE CHART
The Four Basic Steps in Inventing Options

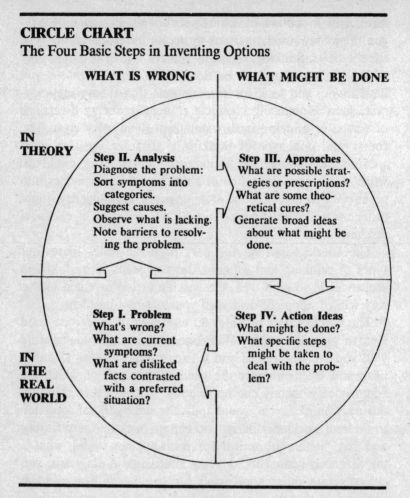

WHAT IS WRONG   WHAT MIGHT BE DONE

IN THEORY

Step II. Analysis
Diagnose the problem:
Sort symptoms into
    categories.
Suggest causes.
Observe what is lacking.
Note barriers to resolv-
    ing the problem.

Step III. Approaches
What are possible strat-
    egies or prescriptions?
What are some theo-
    retical cures?
Generate broad ideas
    about what might be
    done.

Step I. Problem
What's wrong?
What are current
    symptoms?
What are disliked
    facts contrasted
    with a preferred
    situation?

Step IV. Action Ideas
What might be done?
What specific steps
    might be taken to
    deal with the prob-
    lem?

IN THE REAL WORLD

Catholic and Protestant teachers prepare a common workbook
on the history of Northern Ireland for use in the primary
grades of both school systems. The book would present Northern Irish history as seen from different points of view and give
the children exercises that involve role-playing and putting

themselves in other people's shoes. To generate more ideas, you might start with this action suggestion and then search out the theoretical approach that underlies it. You might find such general propositions as:

"There should be some common educational content in the two school systems."

"Catholics and Protestants should work together on small, manageable projects."

"Understanding should be promoted in young children before it is too late."

"History should be taught in ways that illuminate partisan perceptions."

Working with such theory you may be able to invent additional action suggestions, such as a joint Catholic and Protestant film project that presents the history of Northern Ireland as seen through different eyes. Other action ideas might be teacher exchange programs or some common classes for primary-age children in the two systems.

Look through the eyes of different experts. Another way to generate multiple options is to examine your problem from the perspective of different professions and disciplines.

In thinking up possible solutions to a dispute over custody of a child, for example, look at the problem as it might be seen by an educator, a banker, a psychiatrist, a civil rights lawyer, a minister, a nutritionist, a doctor, a feminist, a football coach, or one with some other special point of view. If you are negotiating a business contract, invent options that might occur to a banker, an inventor, a labor leader, a speculator in real estate, a stockbroker, an economist, a tax expert, or a socialist.

You can also combine the use of the Circle Chart with this idea of looking at a problem through the eyes of different experts. Consider in turn how each expert would diagnose the situation, what kinds of approaches each might suggest, and what practical suggestions would follow from those approaches.

Invent agreements of different strengths. You can multiply the number of possible agreements on the table by thinking of "weaker" versions you might want to have on hand in case a sought-for agreement proves beyond reach. If you cannot agree on substance, perhaps you can agree on procedure. If a shoe factory cannot agree with a wholesaler on who should pay for a shipment of damaged shoes, perhaps they can agree to submit the issue to an arbitrator. Similarly, where a permanent agreement is not possible, perhaps a provisional agreement is. At the very least, if you and the other side cannot reach first-order agreement, you can usually reach second-order agreement — that is, agree on where you disagree, so that you both know the issues in dispute, which are not always obvious. The pairs of adjectives below suggest potential agreements of differing "strengths":

STRONGER	WEAKER
Substantive	Procedural
Permanent	Provisional
Comprehensive	Partial
Final	In principle
Unconditional	Contingent
Binding	Nonbinding
First-order	Second-order

Change the scope of a proposed agreement. Consider the possibility of varying not only the strength of the agreement but also its scope. You could, for instance, "fractionate" your problem into smaller and perhaps more manageable units. To a prospective editor for your book, you might suggest: "How about editing the first two chapters for $120, and we'll see how it goes?" Agreements may be partial, involve fewer parties, cover only selected subject matters, apply only to a certain geographical area, or remain in effect for only a limited period of time.

It is also provocative to ask how the subject matter might be enlarged so as to "sweeten the pot" and make agreement more attractive. The dispute between India and Pakistan over the waters of the Indus River became more amenable to settlement when the World Bank entered the discussions; the parties were challenged to invent new irrigation projects, new storage dams, and other engineering works for the benefit of both nations, all to be funded with the assistance of the Bank.

Look for mutual gain

The third major block to creative problem-solving lies in the assumption of a fixed pie: the less for you, the more for me. Rarely if ever is this assumption true. First of all, both sides can always be worse off than they are now. Chess looks like a zero-sum game; if one loses, the other wins — until a dog trots by and knocks over the table, spills the beer, and leaves you both worse off than before.

Even apart from a shared interest in averting joint loss, there almost always exists the possibility of joint gain. This may take the form of developing a mutually advantageous relationship, or of satisfying the interests of each side with a creative solution.

Identify shared interests. In theory it is obvious that shared interests help produce agreement. By definition, inventing an idea which meets shared interests is good for you and good for them. In practice, however, the picture seems less clear. In the middle of a negotiation over price, shared interests may not appear obvious or relevant. How then can looking for shared interests help?

Let's take an example. Suppose you are the manager of an oil refinery. Call it Townsend Oil. The mayor of Pageville,

the city where the refinery is located, has told you he wants
to raise the taxes Townsend Oil pays to Pageville from one
million dollars a year to two million. You have told him that
you think one million a year is quite sufficient. The negotiation stands there: he wants more, you want to pay what you
have been paying. In this negotiation, a typical one in many
ways, where do shared interests come into play?

Let's take a closer look at what the mayor wants. He wants
money — money undoubtedly to pay for city services, a new
civic center, perhaps, and to relieve the ordinary taxpayers.
But the city cannot obtain all the money it needs for now and
for the future just from Townsend Oil. They will look for
money from the petrochemical plant across the street, for example, and, for the future, from new businesses and from the
expansion of existing businesses. The mayor, a businessman
himself, would also like to encourage industrial expansion
and attract new businesses that will provide new jobs and
strengthen Pageville's economy.

What are your company's interests? Given the rapid changes
in the technology of refining oil, and the antiquated condition
of your refinery, you are presently considering a major refur-
bishment and expansion of the plant. You are concerned that
the city may later increase its assessment of the value of the
expanded refinery, thus making taxes even higher. Consider
also that you have been encouraging a plastics plant to locate
itself nearby to make convenient use of your product. Naturally, you worry that the plastics plant will have second
thoughts once they see the city increasing taxes.

The shared interests between the mayor and you now become more apparent. You both agree on the goals of fostering
industrial expansion and encouraging new industries. If you
did some inventing to meet these shared goals, you might come
up with several ideas: a tax holiday of seven years for new
industries, a joint publicity campaign with the Chamber of

Commerce to attract new companies, a reduction in taxes for existing industries that choose to expand. Such ideas might save you money while filling the city's coffers. If on the other hand the negotiation soured the relationship between company and town, both would lose. You might cut back on your corporate contributions to city charities and school athletics. The city might become unreasonably tough on enforcing the building code and other ordinances. Your personal relationship with the city's political and business leaders might grow unpleasant. The relationship between the sides, often taken for granted and overlooked, frequently outweighs in importance the outcome of any particular issue.

As a negotiator, you will almost always want to look for solutions that will leave the other side satisfied as well. If the customer feels cheated in a purchase, the store owner has also failed; he may lose a customer and his reputation may suffer. An outcome in which the other side gets absolutely nothing is worse for you than one which leaves them mollified. In almost every case, your satisfaction depends to a degree on making the other side sufficiently content with an agreement to want to live up to it.

Three points about shared interests are worth remembering. First, shared interests lie latent in every negotiation. They may not be immediately obvious. Ask yourself: Do we have a shared interest in preserving our relationship? What opportunities lie ahead for cooperation and mutual benefit? What costs would we bear if negotiations broke off? Are there common principles, like a fair price, that we both can respect?

Second, shared interests are opportunities, not godsends. To be of use, you need to make something out of them. It helps to make a shared interest explicit and to formulate it as a shared *goal*. In other words, make it concrete and future-oriented. As manager of Townsend Oil, for example, you could set a joint goal with the mayor of bringing five new industries into Pageville within three years. The tax holiday for new industries would then represent not a concession by the mayor to you but an action in pursuit of your shared goal.

Third, stressing your shared interests can make the negotiation smoother and more amicable. Passengers in a lifeboat afloat in the middle of the ocean with limited rations will subordinate their differences over food in pursuit of their shared interest in getting to shore.

Dovetail differing interests. Consider once again the two sisters quarreling over an orange. Each sister wanted the orange, so they split it, failing to realize that one wanted only the fruit to eat and the other only the peel for baking. In this case as in many others, a satisfactory agreement is made possible because each side wants *different* things. This is genuinely startling if you think about it. People generally assume that differences between two parties create the problem. Yet differences can also lead to a solution.

Agreement is often based on disagreement. It is as absurd to think, for example, that you should always begin by reaching agreement on the facts as it is for a buyer of stock to try to convince the seller that the stock is likely to go up. If they did agree that the stock would go up, the seller would probably not sell. What makes a deal likely is that the buyer believes the price will go up and the seller believes it will go down. The difference in belief provides the basis for a deal.

Many creative agreements reflect this principle of reaching agreement through differences. Differences in interests and belief make it possible for an item to be high benefit to you, yet low cost to the other side. Consider the nursery rhyme:

> Jack Sprat could eat no fat
> His wife could eat no lean,
> And so betwixt them both
> They licked the platter clean.

The kinds of differences that best lend themselves to dove-tailing are differences in interests, in beliefs, in the value placed on time, in forecasts, and in aversion to risk.

Any difference in interests? The following brief checklist suggests common variations in interest to look for:

ONE PARTY CARES MORE ABOUT:	THE OTHER PARTY CARES MORE ABOUT:
form	substance
economic considerations	political considerations
internal considerations	external considerations
symbolic considerations	practical considerations
immediate future	more distant future
ad hoc results	the relationship
hardware	ideology
progress	respect for tradition
precedent	this case
prestige, reputation	results
political points	group welfare

Different beliefs? If I believe I'm right, and you believe you're right, we can take advantage of this difference in be-liefs. We may both agree to have an impartial arbitrator settle the issue, each confident of victory. If two factions of the union leadership cannot agree on a certain wage proposal, they can agree to submit the issue to a membership vote.

Different values placed on time? You may care more about the present while the other side cares more about the future. In the language of business, you discount future value at dif-ferent rates. An installment plan works on this principle. The buyer is willing to pay a higher price for the car if he can pay later; the seller is willing to accept payment later if he gets a higher price.

Different forecasts? In a salary negotiation between an ag-ing baseball star and a major league baseball team, the player may expect to win a lot of games while the team owner has the opposite expectation. Taking advantage of these different expectations, they can both agree on a base salary of $100,000 plus $50,000 if the player pitches so well that on the average he permits less than three earned runs per game.

Differences in aversion to risk? One last kind of difference which you may capitalize on is aversion to risk. Take, for example, the issue of deep-seabed mining in the Law of the Sea negotiations. How much should the mining companies pay the international community for the privilege of mining? The mining companies care more about avoiding big losses than they do about making big gains. For them deep-seabed mining is a major investment. They want to reduce the risk. The international community, on the other hand, is concerned with revenue. If some company is going to make a lot of money out of "the common heritage of mankind," the rest of the world wants a generous share.

In this difference lies the potential for a bargain advantageous to both sides. Risk can be traded for revenue. Exploiting this difference in aversion to risk, the proposed treaty provides for charging the companies low rates until they recover their investment — in other words, while their risk is high — and much higher rates thereafter, when their risk is low.

Ask for their preferences. One way to dovetail interests is to invent several options all equally acceptable to you and ask the other side which one they prefer. You want to know what is preferable, not necessarily what is acceptable. You can then take that option, work with it some more, and again present two or more variants, asking which one they prefer. In this way, without anyone's making a decision, you can improve a plan until you can find no more joint gains. For example, the agent for the baseball star might ask the team owner: "What meets your interests better, a salary of $175,000 a year for four years, or $200,000 a year for three years? The latter? OK, how about between that and $180,000 a year for three years with a $50,000 bonus in each year if Luis pitches better than a 3.00 ERA?"

If dovetailing had to be summed up in one sentence, it would be: Look for items that are of low cost to you and high benefit to them, and vice versa. Differences in interests, priorities, beliefs, forecasts, and attitudes toward risk all make dovetailing possible. A negotiator's motto could be *"Vive la différence!"*

Make their decision easy

Since success for you in a negotiation depends upon the other side's making a decision you want, you should do what you can to make that decision an easy one. Rather than make things difficult for the other side, you want to confront them with a choice that is as painless as possible. Impressed with the merits of their own case, people usually pay too little attention to ways of advancing their case by taking care of interests on the other side. To overcome the shortsightedness that results from looking too narrowly at one's immediate self-interest, you will want to put yourself in their shoes. Without some option that appeals to them, there is likely to be no agreement at all.

Whose shoes? Are you trying to influence a single negotiator, an absent boss, or some committee or other collective decision-making body? You cannot negotiate successfully with an abstraction like "Houston" or "the University of California." Instead of trying to persuade "the insurance company" to make a decision, it is wiser to focus your efforts on getting one claims agent to make a recommendation. However complex the other side's decisional process may seem, you will understand it better if you pick one person — probably the person with whom you are dealing — and see how the problem looks from his or her point of view.

By focusing on one person you are not ignoring complexities. Rather, you are handling them by understanding how they impinge on the person with whom you are negotiating. You may come to appreciate your negotiating role in a new light, and see your job, for example, as strengthening that person's hand or giving her arguments that she will need to persuade others to go along. One British ambassador described his job as "helping my opposite number get new instructions." If you place yourself firmly in the shoes of your opposite number, you will understand his problem and what kind of options might solve it.

What decision? In Chapter 2 we discussed how one can understand the other side's interests by analyzing their presently perceived choice. Now you are trying to generate options that will so change their choice that they might then decide in a way satisfactory to you. Your task is to give them not a problem but an answer, to give them not a tough decision but an easy one. It is crucial in that process to focus your attention on the content of the decision itself. That decision is often impeded by uncertainty.

Frequently you want as much as you can get, but you yourself do not know how much that is. You are likely to say, in effect, "Come up with something and I will tell you if it is enough." That may seem reasonable to you, but when you look at it from the other's point of view, you will understand the need to invent a more appealing request. For whatever they do or say, you are likely to consider that merely a floor — and ask for more. Requesting the other side to be "more forthcoming" will probably not produce a decision you want.

Many negotiators are uncertain whether they are asking for words or for performance. Yet the distinction is critical. If it is performance you want, do not add something for "negotiating room." If you want a horse to jump a fence, don't raise the fence. If you want to sell a soft drink from a vending machine for thirty-five cents, don't mark the price at fifty cents to give yourself room to negotiate.

Most of the time you will want a promise — an agreement. Take pencil and paper in hand and try drafting a few possible agreements. It is never too early in a negotiation to start drafting as an aid to clear thinking. Prepare multiple versions, starting with the simplest possible. What are some terms that the other party could sign, terms that would be attractive to them as well as to you? Can you reduce the number of people whose approval would be required? Can you formulate an agreement that will be easy for them to implement? The other side will take into account difficulties in carrying out an agreement; you should too.

It is usually easier, for example, to refrain from doing something not being done than to stop action already underway. And it is easier to cease doing something than to undertake an entirely new course of action. If workers want music on the job, it will be easier for the company to agree not to interfere for a few weeks with an experimental employee-run program of playing records than for the company to agree to run such a program.

Because most people are strongly influenced by their notions of legitimacy, one effective way to develop solutions easy for the other side to accept is to shape them so that they will appear legitimate. The other side is more likely to accept a solution if it seems the right thing to do — right in terms of being fair, legal, honorable, and so forth.

Few things facilitate a decision as much as precedent. Search for it. Look for a decision or statement that the other side may have made in a similar situation, and try to base a proposed agreement on it. This provides an objective standard for your request and makes it easier for them to go along. Recognizing their probable desire to be consistent, and thinking about what they have done or said, will help you generate options acceptable to you that also take their point of view into account.

Making threats is not enough. In addition to the content of the decision you would like them to make, you will want to consider from their point of view the consequences of following that decision. If you were they, what results would you most fear? What would you hope for?

We often try to influence others by threats and warnings of what will happen if they do not decide as we would like. Offers are usually more effective. Concentrate both on making them aware of the consequences they can expect if they do decide as you wish and on improving those consequences from their point of view. How can you make your offers more credible? What are some specific things that they might like? Would they like to be given credit for having made the final proposal? Would they like to make the announcement? What can you invent that might be attractive to them but low in cost to yourself?

To evaluate an option from the other side's point of view, consider how they might be criticized if they adopted it. Write out a sentence or two illustrating what the other side's most powerful critic might say about the decision you are thinking of asking for. Then write out a couple of sentences with which the other side might reply in defense. Such an exercise will help you appreciate the restraints within which the other side is negotiating. It should help you generate options that will adequately meet their interests so that they can make a decision that meets yours.

A final test of an option is to write it out in the form of a "yesable proposition." Try to draft a proposal to which their responding with the single word "yes" would be sufficient, realistic, and operational. When you can do so, you have reduced the risk that your immediate self-interest has blinded you to the necessity of meeting concerns of the other side.

*

In a complex situation, creative inventing is an absolute necessity. In any negotiation it may open doors and produce a range of potential agreements satisfactory to each side. Therefore, generate many options before selecting among them. Invent first; decide later. Look for shared interests and differing interests to dovetail. And seek to make their decision easy.

5 | Insist on Objective Criteria

However well you understand the interests of the other side, however ingeniously you invent ways of reconciling interests, however highly you value an ongoing relationship, you will almost always face the harsh reality of interests that conflict. No talk of "win-win" strategies can conceal that fact. You want the rent to be lower; the landlord wants it to be higher. You want the goods delivered tomorrow; the supplier would rather deliver them next week. You definitely prefer the large office with the view; so does your partner. Such differences cannot be swept under the rug.

Deciding on the basis of will is costly

Typically, negotiators try to resolve such conflicts by positional bargaining — in other words, by talking about what they are willing and unwilling to accept. One negotiator may demand substantive concessions simply because he insists upon them: "The price is $50 and that's that." Another may make a generous offer, hoping to gain approval or friendship. Whether the situation becomes a contest over who can be the most stubborn or a contest over who can be the most generous, this negotiating process focuses on what each side is willing to agree to. The outcome results from the interaction of two human wills — almost as if the negotiators were living on a desert island, with no history, no customs, and no moral standards.

As discussed in Chapter 1, trying to reconcile differences on the basis of will has serious costs. No negotiation is likely to be efficient or amicable if you pit your will against theirs, and either you have to back down or they do. And whether you are choosing a place to eat, organizing a business, or negotiating custody of a child, you are unlikely to reach a wise agreement as judged by any objective standard if you take no such standard into account.

If trying to settle differences of interest on the basis of will has such high costs, the solution is to negotiate on some basis *independent* of the will of either side — that is, on the basis of objective criteria.

The case for using objective criteria

Suppose you have entered into a fixed-price construction contract for your house that calls for reinforced concrete foundations but fails to specify how deep they should be. The contractor suggests two feet. You think five feet is closer to the usual depth for your type of house.

Now suppose the contractor says: "I went along with you on steel girders for the roof. It's your turn to go along with me on shallower foundations." No owner in his right mind would yield. Rather than horse-trade, you would insist on deciding the issue in terms of objective safety standards. "Look, maybe I'm wrong. Maybe two feet is enough. What I want are foundations strong and deep enough to hold up the building safely. Does the government have standard specifications for these soil conditions? How deep are the foundations of other buildings in this area? What is the earthquake risk here? Where do you suggest we look for standards to resolve this question?"

It is no easier to build a good contract than it is to build strong foundations. If relying on objective standards applies so clearly to a negotiation between the house owner and a contractor, why not to business deals, collective bargaining, legal settlements, and international negotiations? Why not insist that a negotiated price, for example, be based on some standard such as market value, replacement cost, depreciated book value, or competitive prices, instead of whatever the seller demands?

In short, the approach is to commit yourself to reaching a solution based on principle, not pressure. Concentrate on the merits of the problem, not the mettle of the parties. Be open to reason, but closed to threats.

Principled negotiation produces wise agreements amicably and efficiently. The more you bring standards of fairness, efficiency, or scientific merit to bear on your particular problem, the more likely you are to produce a final package that is wise and fair. The more you and the other side refer to precedent and community practice, the greater your chance of benefiting from past experience. And an agreement consistent with precedent is less vulnerable to attack. If a lease contains standard terms or if a sales contract conforms to practice in the industry, there is less risk that either negotiator will feel that he was harshly treated or will later try to repudiate the agreement.

A constant battle for dominance threatens a relationship; principled negotiation protects it. It is far easier to deal with people when both of you are discussing objective standards for settling a problem instead of trying to force each other to back down.

Approaching agreement through discussion of objective criteria also reduces the number of commitments that each side must make and then unmake as they move toward agreement. In positional bargaining, negotiators spend much of the time defending their position and attacking the other side's.

People using objective criteria tend to use time more efficiently talking about possible standards and solutions.

Independent standards are even more important to efficiency when more parties are involved. In such cases positional bargaining is difficult at best. It requires coalitions among parties; and the more parties who have agreed on a position, the more difficult it becomes to change that position. Similarly, if each negotiator has a constituency or has to clear a position with a higher authority, the task of adopting positions and then changing them becomes time-consuming and difficult.

An episode during the Law of the Sea Conference illustrates the merits of using objective criteria. At one point, India, representing the Third World bloc, proposed an initial fee for companies mining in the deep seabed of $60 million per site. The United States rejected the proposal, suggesting there be no initial fee. Both sides dug in; the matter became a contest of will.

Then someone discovered that the Massachusetts Institute of Technology (MIT) had developed a model for the economics of deep-seabed mining. This model, gradually accepted by the parties as objective, provided a way of evaluating the impact of any fee proposal on the economics of mining. When the Indian representative asked about the effect of his proposal, he was shown how the tremendous fee he proposed — payable five years before the mine would generate any revenue — would make it virtually impossible for a company to mine. Impressed, he announced that he would reconsider his position. On the other side, the MIT model helped educate the American representatives, whose information on the subject had been mostly limited to that provided by the mining companies. The model indicated that some initial fee was economically feasible. As a result, the U.S. also changed its position.

No one backed down; no one appeared weak — just reasonable. After a lengthy negotiation, the parties reached a tentative agreement that was mutually satisfactory.

The MIT model increased the chance of agreement and decreased costly posturing. It led to a better solution, one that would both attract companies to do mining *and* generate considerable revenue for the nations of the world. The existence of an objective model able to forecast the consequences of any proposal helped convince the parties that the tentative agreement they reached was fair. This in turn strengthened relationships among the negotiators and made it more likely an agreement would endure.

Developing objective criteria

Carrying on a principled negotiation involves two questions: How do you develop objective criteria, and how do you use them in negotiating?

Whatever method of negotiation you use, you will do better if you prepare in advance. This certainly holds true of principled negotiation. So develop some alternative standards beforehand and think through their application to your case.

Fair standards. You will usually find more than one objective criterion available as a basis for agreement. Suppose, for example, your car is demolished and you file a claim with an insurance company. In your discussion with the adjuster, you might take into account such measures of the car's value as (1) the original cost of the car less depreciation; (2) what the car could have been sold for; (3) the standard "blue book" value for a car of that year and model; (4) what it would cost to replace that car with a comparable one; and (5) what a court might award as the value of the car.

In other cases, depending on the issue, you may wish to propose that an agreement be based upon:

market value	what a court would decide
precedent	moral standards
scientific judgment	equal treatment
professional standards	tradition
efficiency	reciprocity
costs	etc.

At a minimum, objective criteria need to be independent of each side's will. Ideally, to assure a wise agreement, objective criteria should be not only independent of will but also both legitimate and practical. In a boundary dispute, for example, you may find it easier to agree on a physically salient feature such as a river than on a line three yards to the east of the riverbank.

Objective criteria should apply, at least in theory, to both sides. You can thus use the test of reciprocal application to tell you whether a proposed criterion is fair and independent of either party's will. If a real estate agency selling you a house offers a standard form contract, you would be wise to ask if that is the same standard form they use when *they* buy a house. In the international arena, the principle of self-determination is notorious for the number of peoples who insist on it as a fundamental right but deny its applicability to those on the other side. Consider the Middle East, Northern Ireland, or Cyprus as just three examples.

Fair procedures. To produce an outcome independent of will, you can use either fair standards for the substantive question or fair procedures for resolving the conflicting interests. Consider, for example, the age-old way to divide a piece of cake between two children: one cuts and the other chooses. Neither can complain about an unfair division.

This simple procedure was used in the Law of the Sea negotiations, one of the most complex negotiations ever undertaken. At one point, the issue of how to allocate mining sites in the deep seabed deadlocked the negotiation. Under the terms of the draft agreement, half the sites were to be mined by private companies, the other half by the Enterprise, a mining organization to be owned by the United Nations. Since the private mining companies from the rich nations had the technology and the expertise to choose the best sites, the poorer nations feared the less knowledgeable Enterprise would receive a bad bargain.

The solution devised was to agree that a private company seeking to mine the seabed would present the Enterprise with *two* proposed mining sites. The Enterprise would pick one site for itself and grant the company a license to mine the other. Since the company would not know which site it would get, it would have an incentive to make both sites as promising as possible. This simple procedure thus harnessed the company's superior expertise for mutual gain.

A variation on the procedure of "one cuts, the other chooses" is for the parties to negotiate what they think is a fair arrangement before they go on to decide their respective roles in it. In a divorce negotiation, for example, before deciding which parent will get custody of the children, the parents might agree on the visiting rights of the other parent. This gives both an incentive to agree on visitation rights each will think fair.

As you consider procedural solutions, look at other basic means of settling differences: taking turns, drawing lots, letting someone else decide, and so on.

Frequently, taking turns presents the best way for heirs to divide a large number of heirlooms left to them collectively. Afterwards, they can do some trading if they want. Or they can make the selection tentative so they see how it comes out before committing themselves to accept it. Drawing lots, flipping a coin, and other forms of chance have an inherent fairness. The results may be unequal, but each side had an equal opportunity.

Letting someone else play a key role in a joint decision is a well-established procedure with almost infinite variations. The parties can agree to submit a particular question to an expert for advice or decision. They can ask a mediator to help them reach a decision. Or they can submit the matter to an arbitrator for an authoritative and binding decision.

Professional baseball, for example, uses "last-best-offer arbitration" to settle player salary disputes. The arbitrator must choose between the last offer made by one side and the last offer made by the other. The theory is that this procedure puts pressure on the parties to make their proposals more reasonable. In baseball, and in states where this form of arbitration is compulsory for certain public employee disputes, it does seem to produce more settlements than in comparable circumstances where there is a commitment to conventional arbitration; those parties who don't settle, however, sometimes give the arbitrator an unpleasant choice between two extreme offers.

Negotiating with objective criteria

Having identified some objective criteria and procedures, how do you go about discussing them with the other side?

Negotiating on the merits has three basic elements:

1. Frame each issue as a joint search for objective criteria.
2. Reason and be open to reason as to which standards are most appropriate and how they should be applied.
3. Never yield to pressure, only to principle.

In short, focus on objective criteria firmly but flexibly.

Frame each issue as a joint search for objective criteria. If you are negotiating to buy a house, you might start off by saying: "Look, you want a high price and I want a low one. Let's figure out what a *fair* price would be. What objective standards might be most relevant?" You and the other side may have conflicting interests, but the two of you now have a shared goal: to determine a fair price. You might begin by suggesting one or more criteria yourself — the cost of the house adjusted for depreciation and inflation, recent sale prices of similar houses in the neighborhood, or an independent appraisal — and then invite the seller's suggestions.

Ask "What's your theory?" If the seller starts by giving you a position, such as "The price is $55,000," ask for the theory behind that price: "How did you arrive at that figure?" Treat the problem as though the seller too is looking for a fair price based on objective criteria.

Agree first on principles. Before even considering possible terms, you may want to agree on the standard or standards to apply.

Each standard the other side proposes becomes a lever you can then use to persuade them. Your case will have more impact if it is presented in terms of their criteria, and they will find it difficult to resist applying their criteria to the problem. "You say Mr. Jones sold the house next door for $60,000. Your theory is that this house should be sold for what comparable houses in the neighborhood are going for, am I right? In that case, let's look at what the house on the corner of Ellsworth and Oxford and the one at Broadway and Dana were sold for." What makes conceding particularly difficult is having to accept someone else's proposal. If they suggested the standard, deferring to it is not an act of weakness but an act of strength, of carrying out their word.

Reason and be open to reason. What makes the negotiation a *joint* search is that, however much you may have prepared various objective criteria, you come to the table with an open mind. In most negotiations, people use precedent and other objective standards simply as arguments in support of a position. A policemen's union might, for example, insist upon a raise of a certain amount and then justify their position with arguments about what police in other cities make. This use of standards usually only digs people even deeper into their position.

Going one step further, some people begin by announcing that their position is an issue of principle and refuse even to consider the other side's case. "It's a matter of principle" becomes a battle cry in a holy war over ideology. Practical differences escalate into principled ones, further locking in the negotiators rather than freeing them.

This is emphatically *not* what is meant by principled negotiation. Insisting that an agreement be based on objective criteria does not mean insisting that it be based solely on the criterion *you* advance. One standard of legitimacy does not preclude the existence of others. What the other side believes to be fair may not be what you believe to be fair. You should behave like a judge; although you may be predisposed to one side (in this case, your own) you should be willing to respond to reasons for applying another standard or for applying a standard differently. When each party is advancing a different standard, look for an objective basis for deciding between them, such as which standard has been used by the parties in the past or which standard is more widely applied. Just as the substantive issue itself should not be settled on the basis of will, neither should the question of which standard applies.

In a given case there may be two standards (such as market value and depreciated cost) which produce different results, but which both parties agree seem equally legitimate. In that case, splitting the difference or otherwise compromising between the results suggested by the two objective standards is perfectly legitimate. The outcome is still independent of the will of the parties.

If, however, after a thorough discussion of the merits of an issue you still cannot accept their proposed criteria as the most appropriate, you might suggest putting them to a test.

Agree on someone you both regard as fair and give him or her a list of the proposed criteria. Ask the person to decide which are the fairest or most appropriate for your situation. Since objective criteria are supposed to be legitimate and because legitimacy implies acceptance by a great many people, this is a fair thing to ask. You are not asking the third party to settle your substantive dispute — just to give you advice on what standard to use in settling it.

The difference between seeking agreement on the appropriate principles for deciding a matter and using principles simply as arguments to support positions is sometimes subtle, but always significant. A principled negotiator is open to reasoned persuasion on the merits; a positional bargainer is not. It is the combination of openness to reason with insistence on a solution based on objective criteria that makes principled negotiation so persuasive and so effective at getting the other side to play.

Never yield to pressure. Consider once again the example of negotiating with the contractor. What if he offers to hire your brother-in-law on the condition that you give in on the depth of the foundations? You would probably answer, "A job for my brother-in-law has nothing to do with whether the house will be safely supported on a foundation of that depth." What if the contractor then threatens to charge you a higher price? You would answer the same way: "We'll settle that question on the merits too. Let's see what other contractors charge for this kind of work," or "Bring me your cost figures and we'll work out a fair profit margin." If the contractor replies, "Come on, you trust me, don't you?" you would respond: "Trust is an entirely separate matter. The issue is how deep the foundations have to be to make the house safe."

Pressure can take many forms: a bribe, a threat, a manipulative appeal to trust, or a simple refusal to budge. In all these cases, the principled response is the same: invite them to state their reasoning, suggest objective criteria you think apply, and refuse to budge except on this basis. Never yield to pressure, only to principle.

Who will prevail? In any given case, it is impossible to say, but in general you will have an edge. For in addition to your willpower, you also have the power of legitimacy and the persuasiveness of remaining open to reason. It will be easier for you to resist making an arbitrary concession than it will be for them to resist advancing some objective standards. A refusal to yield except in response to sound reasons is an easier position to defend — publicly and privately — than is a refusal to yield combined with a refusal to advance sound reasons.

At the least, you will usually prevail on the question of process; you can usually shift the process from positional bargaining to a search for objective criteria. In this sense principled negotiation is a dominant strategy over positional bargaining. One who insists that negotiation be based on the merits can bring others around to playing that game, since that becomes the only way to advance their substantive interests.

On substance, too, you are likely to do well. Particularly for those who might otherwise be browbeaten by a positional bargainer, principled negotiation allows you to hold your own and still be fair. Principle serves as your hardhearted partner who will not let you yield to pressure. It is a form of "right makes might."

If the other side truly will not budge and will not advance a persuasive basis for their position, then there is no further negotiation. You now have a choice like the one you face when you walk into a store which has a fixed, nonnegotiable price on what you want to buy. You can take it or leave it. Before leaving it you should see if you have overlooked some objective standard that makes their offer a fair one. If you find such a standard and if you would rather reach agreement on that basis than have no agreement, do so. The availability of that relevant standard avoids the cost of giving in to an arbitrary position.

If there is no give in their position and you find no principled basis for accepting it, you should assess what you might gain by accepting their unjustified position rather than going to your best alternative. You should weigh that substantive benefit against the benefit to your reputation as a principled negotiator that could come from walking away.

Shifting discussion in a negotiation from the question of what the other side is willing to do to the question of how the matter ought to be decided does not end argument, nor does it guarantee a favorable result. It does, however, provide a strategy you can vigorously pursue without the high costs of positional bargaining.

"It's company policy"

Let's look at a real case where one party used positional bargaining and the other principled negotiation. Tom, one of our colleagues, had his parked car totally destroyed by a dump truck. The car was covered by insurance, but the exact amount Tom could recover remained for him to work out with the insurance adjuster.

INSURANCE ADJUSTER	TOM
We have studied your case and we have decided the policy applies. That means you're entitled to a settlement of $3,300.	
	I see. How did you reach that figure?
That's how much we decided the car was worth.	
	I understand, but what standard did you use to determine that

How much are you asking for?

amount? Do you know where I can buy a comparable car for that much?

Whatever I'm entitled to under the policy. I found a second-hand car just about like it for $3,850. Adding the sales and excise tax, it would come to about $4,000.

$4,000! That's too much!

I'm not asking for $4,000 or $3,000 or $5,000, but for fair compensation. Do you agree that it's only fair I get enough to replace the car?

OK, I'll offer you $3,500. That's the highest I can go. Company policy.

How does the company figure that?

Look, $3,500 is all you'll get. Take it or leave it.

$3,500 may be fair. I don't know. I certainly understand your position if you're bound by company policy. But unless you can state objectively why that amount is what I'm entitled to, I think I'll do better in court. Why don't we study the matter and talk again? Is Wednesday at eleven a good time to talk?

* * *

OK, Mr. Griffith, I've got an ad here in today's paper offering a '78 Fiesta for $3,400.

I see. What does it say about the mileage?

49,000. Why?

Because mine only had 25,000 miles. How many dollars does that increase the worth in your book?

Let me see . . . $150.

Assuming the $3,400 as one possible base, that brings the figure to $3,550. Does the ad say anything about a radio?

No.

How much extra for that in your book?

$125.

How much for air conditioning?

* * *

A half-hour later Tom walked out with a check for $4,012.

III | Yes, But...

6 | What If They Are More Powerful?

**(Develop Your BATNA —
Best Alternative To a Negotiated Agreement)**

Of what use is talking about interests, options, and standards if the other side has a stronger bargaining position? What do you do if the other side is richer or better connected, or if they have a larger staff or more powerful weapons?

No method can guarantee success if all the leverage lies on the other side. No book on gardening can teach you to grow lilies in a desert or cactus in a swamp. If you enter an antique store to buy a sterling silver George IV tea set worth thousands of dollars and all you have is one hundred-dollar bill, you should not expect skillful negotiation to overcome the difference. In any negotiation there exist realities that are hard to change. In response to power, the most any method of negotiation can do is to meet two objectives: *first,* to protect you against making an agreement you should reject and *second,* to help you make the most of the assets you do have so that any agreement you reach will satisfy your interests as well as possible. Let's take each objective in turn.

Protecting yourself

When you are trying to catch an airplane your goal may seem tremendously important; looking back on it, you see you could have caught the next plane. Negotiation will often present you with a similar situation. You will worry, for instance, about failing to reach agreement on an important business deal in which you have invested a great deal of yourself. Under these conditions, a major danger is that you will be too accommodating to the views of the other side — too quick to go along. The siren song of "Let's all agree and put an end to this" becomes persuasive. You may end up with a deal you should have rejected.

The costs of using a bottom line. Negotiators commonly try to protect themselves against such an outcome by establishing in advance the worst acceptable outcome — their "bottom line." If you are buying, a bottom line is the highest price you would pay. If you are selling, a bottom line is the lowest amount you would accept. You and your spouse might, for example, ask $100,000 for your house and agree between yourselves to accept no offer below $80,000.

Having a bottom line makes it easier to resist pressure and temptations of the moment. In the house example, it might be impossible for a buyer to pay more than $72,000; everyone involved may know that you bought the house last year for only $50,000. In this situation, where you have the power to produce agreement and the buyer does not, the brokers and anyone else in the room may turn to you. Your predetermined bottom line may save you from making a decision you would later regret.

If there is more than one person on your side, jointly adopting a bottom line helps ensure that no one will indicate to the other side that you might settle for less. It limits the authority of a lawyer, broker, or other agent. "Get the best price you can, but you are not authorized to sell for less than $80,000," you might say. If your side is a loose coalition of newspaper unions negotiating with an association of publishers, agreement on a bottom line reduces the risk that one union will be split off by offers from the other side.

But the protection afforded by adopting a bottom line involves high costs. It limits your ability to benefit from what you learn during negotiation. By definition, a bottom line is a position that is not to be changed. To that extent you have shut your ears, deciding in advance that nothing the other party says could cause you to raise or lower that bottom line.

A bottom line also inhibits imagination. It reduces the incentive to invent a tailor-made solution which would reconcile differing interests in a way more advantageous for both you and them. Almost every negotiation involves more than one variable. Rather than simply selling your place for $80,000, you might serve your interests better by settling for $67,500 with a first refusal on resale, a delayed closing, the right to use the barn for storage for two years, and an option to buy back two acres of the pasture. If you insist on a bottom line, you are not likely to explore an imaginative solution like this. A bottom line — by its very nature rigid — is almost certain to be *too* rigid.

Moreover, a bottom line is likely to be set too high. Suppose you are sitting around the breakfast table with your family trying to decide the lowest price you should accept for your house. One family member suggests $50,000. Another replies, "We should get at least $70,000." A third chimes in, "$70,000 for *our* house? That would be a steal. It's worth at least $100,000." Who sitting at the table will object, knowing they will benefit from a higher price? Once decided upon, such a bottom line may be hard to change and may prevent your selling the house for years. Under other circumstances a bottom line may be too low; rather than selling at such a figure, you would have been better off renting.

In short, while adopting a bottom line may protect you from accepting a very bad agreement, it may keep you both from inventing and from agreeing to a solution it would be wise to accept. An arbitrarily selected figure is no measure of what you should accept.

Is there an alternative to the bottom line? Is there a measure for agreements that will protect you against both accepting an agreement you should reject and rejecting an agreement you should accept? There is.

Know your BATNA. When a family is deciding on the minimum price for their house, the right question for them to ask is not what they "ought" to be able to get, but what they will do if by a certain time they have not sold the house. Will they keep it on the market indefinitely? Will they rent it, tear it down, turn the land into a parking lot, let someone else live in it rent-free on condition they paint it, or what? Which of those options is most attractive, all things considered? And how does that option compare with the best offer received for the house? It may be that one of those alternatives is more attractive than selling the house for $80,000. On the other hand, selling the house for as little as $62,000 may be better than holding on to it indefinitely. It is most unlikely that any arbitrarily selected bottom line truly reflects the family's interests.

The reason you negotiate is to produce something better than the results you can obtain without negotiating. What are those results? What is that alternative? What is your BATNA — your Best Alternative To a Negotiated Agreement? *That* is the standard against which any proposed agreement should be measured. That is the only standard which can protect you both from accepting terms that are too unfavorable and from rejecting terms it would be in your interest to accept.

Your BATNA not only is a better measure but also has the advantage of being flexible enough to permit the exploration of imaginative solutions. Instead of ruling out any solution which does not meet your bottom line, you can compare a proposal with your BATNA to see whether it better satisfies your interests.

The insecurity of an unknown BATNA. If you have not thought carefully about what you will do if you fail to reach an agreement, you are negotiating with your eyes closed. You may, for instance, be too optimistic and assume that you have many other choices: other houses for sale, other buyers for your secondhand car, other plumbers, other jobs available, other wholesalers, and so on. Even when your alternative is fixed, you may be taking too rosy a view of the consequences of not reaching agreement. You may not be appreciating the full agony of a lawsuit, a contested divorce, a strike, an arms race, or a war.

One frequent mistake is psychologically to see your alternatives in the aggregate. You may be telling yourself that if you do not reach agreement on a salary for this job, you could always go to California, or go South, or go back to school, or write, or work on a farm, or live in Paris, or do something else. In your mind you are likely to find the sum of these options more attractive than working for a specific salary in a particular job. The difficulty is that you cannot have the sum total of all those other options; if you fail to reach agreement, you will have to choose just one.

In most circumstances, however, the greater danger is that you are *too* committed to reaching agreement. Not having developed any alternative to a negotiated solution, you are unduly pessimistic about what would happen if negotiations broke off.

As valuable as knowing your BATNA may be, you may hesitate to explore alternatives. You hope this buyer or the next will make you an attractive offer for the house. You may avoid facing the question of what you will do if no agreement is reached. You may think to yourself, "Let's negotiate first and see what happens. If things don't work out, then I'll figure out what to do." But having at least a tentative answer to the question is absolutely essential if you are to conduct your negotiations wisely. Whether you should or should not agree on something in a negotiation depends entirely upon the attractiveness to you of the best available alternative.

Formulate a trip wire. Although your BATNA is the true measure by which you should judge any proposed agreement, you may want another test as well. In order to give you early warning that the content of a possible agreement is beginning to run the risk of being too unattractive, it is useful to identify one far from perfect agreement that is better than your BATNA. Before accepting any agreement worse than this trip-wire package, you should take a break and reexamine the situation. Like a bottom line, a trip wire can limit the authority of an agent. "Don't sell for less than $79,000, the price I paid plus interest, until you've talked to me."

A trip wire should provide you with some margin in reserve. If after reaching the standard reflected in your trip wire you decide to call in a mediator, you have left him with something on your side to work with. You still have some room to move.

Making the most of your assets

Protecting yourself against a bad agreement is one thing. Making the most of the assets you have in order to produce a good agreement is another. How do you do this? Again the answer lies in your BATNA.

The better your BATNA, the greater your power. People think of negotiating power as being determined by resources like wealth, political connections, physical strength, friends, and military might. In fact, the relative negotiating power of two parties depends primarily upon how attractive to each is the option of not reaching agreement.

Consider a wealthy tourist who wants to buy a small brass pot for a modest price from a vendor at the Bombay railroad station. The vendor may be poor, but he is likely to know the market. If he does not sell the pot to this tourist, he can sell it to another. From his experience he can estimate when and for how much he could sell it to someone else. The tourist may be wealthy and "powerful," but in this negotiation he will be weak indeed unless he knows approximately how much it would cost and how difficult it would be to find a comparable pot elsewhere. He is almost certain either to miss his chance to buy such a pot or to pay too high a price. The tourist's wealth in no way strengthens his negotiating power. If apparent, it *weakens* his ability to buy the pot at a low price. In order to convert that wealth into negotiating power, the tourist would have to apply it to learn about the price at which he could buy an equally or more attractive brass pot somewhere else.

Think for a moment about how you would feel walking into a job interview with no other job offers — only some uncertain leads. Think how the talk about salary would go. Now contrast that with how you would feel walking in with two other job offers. How would that salary negotiation proceed? The difference is power.

What is true for negotiations between individuals is equally true for negotiations between organizations. The relative negotiating power of a large industry and a small town trying to raise taxes on a factory is determined not by the relative size of their respective budgets, or their political clout, but by each side's best alternative. In one case, a small town negotiated a company with a factory just outside the town limits from a "goodwill" payment of $300,000 a year to one of $2,300,000 a year. How?

The town knew exactly what it would do if no agreement was reached: It would expand the town limits to include the factory and then tax the factory the full residential rate of some $2,500,000 a year. The corporation had committed itself to keeping the factory; it had developed no alternative to reaching agreement. At first glance the corporation seemed to have a great deal of power. It provided most of the jobs in the town, which was suffering economically; a factory shut-down or relocation would devastate the town. And the taxes the corporation was already paying helped provide the salaries of the very town leaders who were demanding more. Yet all of this power, because it was not converted into a good BATNA, proved of little use. Having an attractive BATNA, the small town had more ability to affect the outcome of the negotiation than did one of the world's largest corporations.

Develop your BATNA. Vigorous exploration of what you will do if you do not reach agreement can greatly strengthen your hand. Attractive alternatives are not just sitting there waiting for you; you usually have to develop them. Generating possible BATNAs requires three distinct operations: (1) inventing a list of actions you might conceivably take if no agreement is reached; (2) improving some of the more promising ideas and converting them into practical options; and (3) selecting, tentatively, the one option that seems best.

The first operation is inventing. If, by the end of the month, Company X does not make you a satisfactory job offer, what are some things you might do? Take a job with Company Y? Look in another city? Start a business on your own? What else? For a labor union, alternatives to a negotiated agreement would presumably include calling a strike, working without a contract, giving a sixty-day notice of a strike, asking for a mediator, and calling on union members to "work to rule."

The second stage is to improve the best of your ideas and turn the most promising into real options. If you are thinking about working in Chicago, try to turn that idea into at least one job offer there. With a Chicago job offer in hand (or even having discovered that you are unable to produce one) you are much better prepared to assess the merits of a New York offer. While a labor union is still negotiating, it should convert the ideas of calling in a mediator and of striking into drafts of specific operational decisions ready for execution.

The union might, for instance, take a vote of its membership to authorize a strike if a settlement is not achieved by the time the contract expires.

The final step in developing a BATNA is selecting the best among the options. If you do not reach agreement in the negotiations, which of your realistic options do you now plan to pursue?

Having gone through this effort, you now have a BATNA. Judge every offer against it. The better your BATNA, the greater your ability to improve the terms of any negotiated agreement. Knowing what you are going to do if the negotiation does not lead to agreement will give you additional confidence in the negotiating process. It is easier to break off negotiations if you know where you're going. The greater your willingness to break off negotiations, the more forcefully you can present your interests and the basis on which you believe an agreement should be reached.

The desirability of disclosing your BATNA to the other side depends upon your assessment of the other side's thinking. If your BATNA is extremely attractive — if you have another customer waiting in the next room — it is in your interest to let the other side know. If they think you lack a good alternative when in fact you have one, then you should almost certainly let them know. However, if your best alternative to a negotiated agreement is worse for you than they think, disclosing it will weaken rather than strengthen your hand.

Consider the other side's BATNA. You should also think about the alternatives to a negotiated agreement available to the other side. They may be unduly optimistic about what they can do if no agreement is reached. Perhaps they have a vague notion that they have a great many options and are under the influence of their cumulative total.

The more you can learn of their options, the better prepared you are for negotiation. Knowing their alternatives, you can realistically estimate what you can expect from the negotiation. If they appear to overestimate their BATNA, you will want to lower their expectations.

Their BATNA may be better for them than any fair solution you can imagine. Suppose you are a community group concerned about the potential noxious gases to be emitted by a power plant now under construction. The power company's BATNA is either to ignore your protests altogether or to keep you talking while they finish building the plant. To get them to take your concerns seriously, you may have to file suit seeking to have their construction permit revoked. In other words, if their BATNA is so good they don't see any need to negotiate on the merits, consider what you can do to change it.

If both sides have attractive BATNAs, the best outcome of the negotiation — for both parties — may well be not to reach agreement. In such cases a successful negotiation is one in which you and they amicably and efficiently discover that the best way to advance your respective interests is for each of you to look elsewhere and not to try further to reach agreement.

When the other side is powerful

If the other side has big guns, you do not want to turn a negotiation into a gunfight. The stronger they appear in terms of physical or economic power, the more you benefit by negotiating on the merits. To the extent that they have muscle and you have principle, the larger a role you can establish for principle the better off you are.

Having a good BATNA can help you negotiate on the merits. You can convert such resources as you have into effective negotiating power by developing and improving your BATNA. Apply knowledge, time, money, people, connections, and wits into devising the best solution for you independent of the other side's assent. The more easily and happily you can walk away from a negotiation, the greater your capacity to affect its outcome.

Developing your BATNA thus not only enables you to determine what is a minimally acceptable agreement, it will probably raise that minimum. Developing your BATNA is perhaps the most effective course of action you can take in dealing with a seemingly more powerful negotiator.

7 | What If They Won't Play?

(Use Negotiation Jujitsu)

Talking about interests, options, and standards may be a wise, efficient, and amicable game, but what if the other side won't play? While you try to discuss interests, they may state their position in unequivocal terms. You may be concerned with developing possible agreements to maximize the gains of both parties. They may be attacking your proposals, concerned only with maximizing their own gains. You may attack the problem on its merits; they may attack you. What can you do to turn them away from positions and toward the merits?

There are three basic approaches for focusing their attention on the merits. The first centers on what *you* can do. You yourself can concentrate on the merits, rather than on positions. This method, the subject of this book, is contagious; it holds open the prospect of success to those who will talk about interests, options, and criteria. In effect, you can change the game simply by starting to play a new one.

If this doesn't work and they continue to use positional bargaining, you can resort to a second strategy which focuses on what *they* may do. It counters the basic moves of positional bargaining in ways that direct their attention to the merits. This strategy we call *negotiation jujitsu*.

The third approach focuses on what a *third party* can do. If neither principled negotiation nor negotiation jujitsu gets them to play, consider including a third party trained to focus the discussion on interests, options, and criteria. Perhaps the most effective tool a third party can use in such an effort is the one-text mediation procedure.

The first approach — principled negotiation — has already been discussed. Negotiation jujitsu and the one-text procedure are explained in this chapter. The chapter ends with a dialogue based on an actual landlord-tenant negotiation that illustrates in detail how you might persuade an unwilling party to play, using a combination of principled negotiation and negotiation jujitsu.

Negotiation jujitsu

If the other side announces a firm position, you may be tempted to criticize and reject it. If they criticize your proposal, you may be tempted to defend it and dig yourself in. If they attack you, you may be tempted to defend yourself and counterattack. In short, if they push you hard, you will tend to push back.

Yet if you do, you will end up playing the positional bargaining game. Rejecting their position only locks them in. Defending your proposal only locks *you* in. And defending yourself sidetracks the negotiation into a clash of personalities. You will find yourself in a vicious cycle of attack and defense, and you will waste a lot of time and energy in useless pushing and pulling.

If pushing back does not work, what does? How can you prevent the cycle of action and reaction? *Do not push back.* When they assert their positions, do not reject them. When they attack your ideas, don't defend them. When they attack you, don't counterattack. Break the vicious cycle by refusing to react. Instead of pushing back, sidestep their attack and deflect it against the problem. As in the Oriental martial arts of judo and jujitsu, avoid pitting your strength against theirs directly; instead, use your skill to step aside and turn their strength to your ends. Rather than resisting their force, channel it into exploring interests, inventing options for mutual gain, and searching for independent standards.

How does "negotiation jujitsu" work in practice? How do you sidestep their attack and deflect it against the problem?

Typically their "attack" will consist of three maneuvers: asserting their position forcefully, attacking your ideas, and attacking you. Let's consider how a principled negotiator can deal with each of these.

Don't attack their position, look behind it. When the other side sets forth their position, neither reject it nor accept it. Treat it as one possible option. Look for the interests behind it, seek out the principles which it reflects, and think about ways to improve it.

Let's say you represent an association of teachers striking for higher pay and for seniority as the only criterion in layoffs. The school board has proposed a $1,000 raise across the board plus retention of the right to decide unilaterally who gets laid off. Mine their position for the interests that lie below the surface. "What exactly are the budget trade-offs involved in raising the salary schedule more than $1,000?" "Why do you feel a need to maintain complete control over layoffs?"

Assume every position they take is a genuine attempt to address the basic concerns of each side; ask them how they think it addresses the problem at hand. Treat their position as one option and objectively examine the extent to which it meets the interests of each party, or might be improved to do so. "How will a $1,000 across-the-board increase keep our schools' salaries competitive with others in the area and thus assure that the students will have high-quality teachers?" "How could you satisfy the teachers that your evaluation procedure for layoffs would be fair? We believe that you personally would be fair, but what would happen if you left? How can we leave our livelihoods and our families' well-being up to a potentially arbitrary decision?"

Seek out and discuss the principles underlying the other side's positions. "What is the theory that makes $1,000 a fair salary increase? Is it based on what other schools pay or what others with comparable qualifications make?" "Do you believe that the town's least experienced teachers should be laid off first or the most experienced — who, of course, have higher salaries?"

To direct their attention toward improving the options on the table discuss with them hypothetically what would happen if one of their positions was accepted. In 1970, an American lawyer had a chance to interview President Nasser of Egypt on the subject of the Arab-Israeli conflict. He asked Nasser, "What is it you want Golda Meir to do?"

Nasser replied, "Withdraw!"

"Withdraw?" the lawyer asked.

"Withdraw from every inch of Arab territory!"

"Without a deal? With nothing from you?" the American asked incredulously.

"Nothing. It's our territory. She should promise to withdraw," Nasser replied.

The American asked, "What would happen to Golda Meir if tomorrow morning she appeared on Israeli radio and television and said, 'On behalf of the people of Israel I hereby promise to withdraw from every inch of territory occupied in '67: the Sinai, Gaza, the West Bank, Jerusalem, the Golan Heights. And I want you to know, I have no commitment of any kind from any Arab whatsoever.' "

Nasser burst out laughing, "Oh, would *she* have trouble at home!"

Understanding what an unrealistic option Egypt had been offering Israel may have contributed to Nasser's stated willingness later that day to accept a cease-fire in the war of attrition.

Don't defend your ideas, invite criticism and advice. A lot of time in negotiation is spent criticizing. Rather than resisting the other side's criticism, invite it. Instead of asking them to accept or reject an idea, ask them what's wrong with it. "What concerns of yours would this salary proposal fail to take into account?" Examine their negative judgments to find out their underlying interests and to improve your ideas from their point of view. Rework your ideas in light of what you learn from them, and thus turn criticism from an obstacle in the process of working toward agreement into an essential ingredient of that process. "If I understand you, you're saying you can't afford to give 750 teachers more than a $1,000 across-the-board raise. What if we accept that with the stipulation that any money saved by hiring fewer than 750 full-time teachers will be distributed as a monthly bonus to those teachers who are working?"

Another way to channel criticism in a constructive direction is to turn the situation around and ask for their advice. Ask them what they would do if they were in your position. "If your jobs were at stake, what would you do? Our members are feeling so insecure about their jobs and frustrated by their shrinking dollars they're talking about inviting a militant union in to represent them. If you were leading this association, how would you act?" Thus, you lead them to confront your half of the problem. In doing so, they may be able to invent a solution that meets your concerns. "Part of the problem here seems to be that the teachers feel no one's listening. Would it help to have regular sessions at which teachers could meet with the school board?"

Recast an attack on you as an attack on the problem. When the other side attacks you personally — as frequently happens — resist the temptation to defend yourself or to attack them. Instead, sit back and allow them to let off steam. Listen to them, show you understand what they are saying, and when they have finished, recast their attack on you as an attack on the problem. "When you say that a strike shows we don't care about the children, I hear your concern about the children's education. I want you to know that we share this concern: they are our children and our students. We want the strike to end so we can go back to educating them. What can we both do now to reach an agreement as quickly as possible?"

Ask questions and pause. Those engaged in negotiation jujitsu use two key tools. The first is to use questions instead of statements. Statements generate resistance, whereas questions generate answers. Questions allow the other side to get their points across and let you understand them. They pose challenges and can be used to lead the other side to confront the problem. Questions offer them no target to strike at, no position to attack. Questions do not criticize, they educate. "Do you think it would be better to have teachers cooperating in a process they felt they were participating in, or actively resisting one they felt was imposed on them and failed to take their concerns into account?"

Silence is one of your best weapons. Use it. If they have made an unreasonable proposal or an attack you regard as unjustified, the best thing to do may be to sit there and not say a word.

If you have asked an honest question to which they have provided an insufficient answer, just wait. People tend to feel uncomfortable with silence, particularly if they have doubts about the merits of something they have said. For example, if a teacher's representative asks, "Why shouldn't teachers have a say in layoff policy?" the school board chairman might find himself at a loss: "Layoffs are a purely administrative matter. . . . Well, of course teachers have an interest in layoff policy, but they really aren't the best qualified to know who's a good teacher. . . . Uh, what I mean is . . . ."

Silence often creates the impression of a stalemate which the other side will feel impelled to break by answering your question or coming up with a new suggestion. When you ask questions, pause. Don't take them off the hook by going right on with another question or some comment of your own. Some of the most effective negotiating you will ever do is when you are not talking.

Consider the one-text procedure

You will probably call in a third party only if your own efforts to shift the game from positional bargaining to principled negotiation have failed. The problem you face may be illustrated by a simple story of a negotiation between a husband and wife who plan to build a new house.

The wife is thinking of a two-story house with a chimney and a bay window. The husband is thinking of a modern ranch-style house, with a den and a garage with a lot of storage space. In the process of negotiating, each asks the other a number of questions, like "What are your views on the living room?" and "Do you really insist on having it your way?" Through answering such questions, two separate plans become more and more fixed. They each ask an architect to prepare first a sketch and then more detailed plans, ever more firmly digging themselves into their respective positions. In response to the wife's demand for some flexibility, the husband agrees to reduce the length of the garage by one foot. In response to his insistence on a concession, the wife agrees to give up a back porch which she says she had always wanted, but which did not even appear on her plan. Each argues in support of one plan and against the other. In the process, feelings are hurt and communication becomes difficult. Neither side wants to make a concession since it will likely lead only to requests for more concessions.

This is a classic case of positional bargaining. If you cannot change the process to one of seeking a solution on the merits, perhaps a third party can. More easily than one of those directly involved, a mediator can separate the people from the problem and direct the discussion to interests and options. Further, he or she can often suggest some impartial basis for resolving differences. A third party can also separate inventing from decision-making, reduce the number of decisions required to reach agreement, and help the parties know what they will get when they do decide. One process designed to enable a third party to do all this is known as the one-text procedure.

In the house-designing negotiation between husband and wife, an independent architect is called in and shown the latest plans reflecting the present positions of the husband and the wife. Not all third parties will behave wisely. One architect, for example, might ask the parties for clarification of their positions, press them for a long series of concessions, and make them even more emotionally attached to their particular solutions. But an architect using the one-text procedure would behave differently. Rather than ask about their positions he asks about their interests: not how big a bay window the wife wants, but why she wants it. "Is it for morning sun or afternoon sun? Is it to look out or look in?" He would ask the husband, "Why do you want a garage? What things do you need to store? What do you expect to do in your den? Read? Look at television? Entertain friends? When will you use the den? During the day? Weekends? Evenings?" And so forth.

The architect makes clear he is not asking either spouse to give up a position. Rather, he is exploring the possibility that he might be able to make a recommendation to them — but even that is uncertain. At this stage he is just trying to learn all he can about their needs and interests.

Afterwards, the architect develops a list of interests and needs of the two spouses ("morning sun, open fireplace, comfortable place to read, room for a shop, storage for snowblower and medium-sized car," and so on). He asks each spouse in turn to criticize the list and suggest improvements on it. It is hard to make concessions, but it is easy to criticize.

A few days later the architect returns with a rough floor plan. "Personally, I am dissatisfied with it, but before working on it further I thought I would get your criticisms." The husband might say, "What's wrong with it? Well, for one thing, the bathroom is too far from the bedroom. I don't see enough room for my books. And where would overnight guests sleep?" The wife, too, is asked for her criticism of the first sketch.

A short time later the architect comes back with a second sketch, again asking for criticism. "I've tried to deal with the bathroom problem and the book problem, and also with the idea of using the den as a spare bedroom. What do you think about this?" As the plan takes shape, each spouse will tend to raise those issues most important to him or to her, not trivial details. Without conceding anything, the wife, for example, will want to make sure that the architect fully understands her major needs. No one's ego, not even that of the architect, is committed to any draft. Inventing the best possible reconciliation of their interests within the financial constraints is separated from making decisions and is free of the fear of making an overhasty commitment. Husband and wife do not have to abandon their positions, but they now sit side by side, at least figuratively, jointly critiquing the plans as they take shape and helping the architect prepare a recommendation he may later present to them.

And so it goes, through a third plan, a fourth, and a fifth. Finally, when he feels he can improve it no further, the architect says, "This is the best I can do. I have tried to reconcile your various interests as best I could. Many of the issues I have resolved using standard architectural and engineering solutions, precedent, and the best professional judgment I can bring to bear. Here it is. I recommend you accept this plan."

Each spouse now has only one decision to make: yes or no. In making their decisions they know exactly what they are going to get. And a yes answer can be made contingent on the other side's also saying yes. The one-text procedure not only shifts the game away from positional bargaining, it greatly simplifies the process both of inventing options and of deciding jointly on one.

In other negotiations, who could play the role of the architect? You could invite a third party in to mediate. Or, in negotiations involving more than two parties, a natural third party may be a participant whose interests on this issue lie more in effecting an agreement than in affecting the particular terms.

In many negotiations that someone may be you. For instance, you may be a salesman for a plastics plant negotiating a large order with an industrial customer who makes plastic bottles. The customer may want a special kind of plastic made up for him, but the plant you represent may be reluctant to do the retooling needed for the order. Your commission depends more on effecting an agreement between your customer and your production people than on affecting the terms. Or you may be a legislative assistant for a senator who is more concerned with getting a certain appropriations bill passed than with whether the appropriation is ten million dollars or eleven. Or you may be a manager trying to decide an issue on which each of your two subordinates favors a different course of action; you care more about making a decision both can live with than about which alternative is chosen. In each of these cases, even though you are an active participant, it may be in your best interest to behave as a mediator would and to use the one-text procedure. Mediate your own dispute.

Perhaps the most famous use of the one-text procedure was by the United States at Camp David in September 1978 when mediating between Egypt and Israel. The United States listened to both sides, prepared a draft to which no one was committed, asked for criticism, and improved the draft again and again until the mediators felt they could improve it no further. After thirteen days and some twenty-three drafts, the United States had a text it was prepared to recommend. When President Carter did recommend it, Israel and Egypt accepted. As a mechanical technique for limiting the number of decisions, reducing the uncertainty of each decision, and preventing the parties from getting increasingly locked into their positions, it worked remarkably well.

The one-text procedure is a great help for two-party negotiations involving a mediator. It is almost essential for large multilateral negotiations. One hundred and fifty nations, for example, cannot constructively discuss a hundred and fifty different proposals. Nor can they make concessions contingent upon mutual concessions by everybody else. They need some way to simplify the process of decision-making. The one-text procedure serves that purpose.

You do not have to get anyone's consent to start using the one-text procedure. Simply prepare a draft and ask for criticism. Again, you can change the game simply by starting to play the new one. Even if the other side is not willing to talk to you directly (or vice versa), a third party can take a draft around.

Getting them to play:
The case of Jones Realty and Frank Turnbull

The following real-life example of a negotiation between a landlord and tenant should give you a feel for how you might deal with a party who is reluctant to engage in principled negotiation. It illustrates what it means to change the game by starting to play a new one.

The case in brief. Frank Turnbull rented an apartment in March from Jones Realty for $300 a month. In July, when he and his roommate, Paul, wanted to move out, Turnbull learned that the apartment was under rent control. The maximum legal rent was $233 a month — $67 less than he had been paying.

Disturbed that he had been overcharged, Turnbull called

on Mrs. Jones of Jones Realty to discuss the problem. At first, Mrs. Jones was unreceptive and hostile. She claimed to be right and accused Turnbull of ingratitude and blackmail. After several long negotiating sessions, however, Mrs. Jones agreed to reimburse Turnbull and his roommate. Her tone in the end became friendlier and apologetic.

Throughout, Turnbull used the method of principled negotiation. Presented below is a selection of the exchanges that took place during the negotiation. Each exchange is headed by a stock phrase that a principled negotiator might use in any similar situation. Following each exchange is an analysis of the theory that lies behind it and its impact.

"Please correct me if I'm wrong"

TURNBULL: Mrs. Jones, I've just learned — please correct me if I'm wrong — that our apartment's under rent control. We've been told that the legal maximum rent is $233 a month. Have we been misinformed?

Analysis. The essence of principled negotiation lies in remaining open to persuasion by objective facts and principles. By cautiously treating the objective facts as possibly inaccurate and asking Mrs. Jones to correct them, Turnbull establishes a dialogue based on reason. He invites her to participate by either agreeing with the facts as presented or setting them right. This game makes them two colleagues trying to establish the facts. The confrontation is defused. If Turnbull simply asserted the facts as facts, Mrs. Jones would feel threatened and defensive. She might deny the facts. The negotiation would not start off constructively.

If Turnbull is genuinely mistaken, asking for corrections beforehand will make them easier to accept. To tell Mrs. Jones that these are the facts, only to learn he is wrong, would make him lose face. Worse yet, she would then doubt all the more anything else he says, making it difficult to negotiate.

Making yourself open to correction and persuasion is a pillar in the strategy of principled negotiation. You can convince the other side to be open to the principles and objective facts you suggest only if you show yourself open to the ones they suggest.

"We appreciate what you've done for us"

TURNBULL: Paul and I understand you were doing us a personal favor by renting us this apartment. You were very kind to put in the time and effort, and we appreciate it.

Analysis. Giving personal support to the person on the other side is crucial to separating the people from the problem — separating relationship issues from the substantive merits. By expressing his appreciation of Mrs. Jones's good deeds, Turnbull in effect says, "We have nothing against you personally. We think you're a generous person." He puts himself on her side. He defuses any threat she may feel to her self-image.

Praise and support, moreover, imply that the person will continue to deserve them. After being praised, Mrs. Jones now has a slight emotional investment in Turnbull's approval of her. She has something to lose and as a result may act more conciliatory.

"Our concern is fairness"

TURNBULL: We want to know that we didn't pay any more than we should have. When we're persuaded that the rent paid measures up fairly to the time spent in the apartment, we'll call it even and move out.

Analysis. Turnbull takes a basic stand on principle and announces his intention to stick to it; he must be persuaded on the basis of principle. At the same time, he lets Mrs. Jones know he is open to persuasion along the lines of this principle. She is thus left with little choice but to reason with him in pursuit of her interests.

Turnbull does not take a righteous stand on principle backed up with whatever power he possesses. Not only are his ends principled but also the means he contemplates. His ends, he claims, are a fair balance between rent paid and time spent. If convinced the rent paid is just right for the time spent, he will move out. If the rent paid is excessive, it is only fair that he remain in the apartment until the rent and the time spent are in balance.

"We would like to settle this on the basis not of selfish interest and power but of principle"

MRS. JONES: It's funny you should mention fairness, because what you're really saying is that you and Paul just want money, and that you're going to take advantage of your still being in the apartment to try and get it from us. That really makes me angry. If I had my way, you and Paul would be out of the apartment today.

TURNBULL *(barely controlling his anger)*: I must not be making myself clear. Of course it would be nice if Paul and I got some money. Of course, we could try and stay here in the apartment until you got us evicted. But that's not the point, Mrs. Jones.

More important to us than making a few dollars here or there is the feeling of being fairly treated. No one likes to feel cheated. And if we made this a matter of who's got the power and refused to move, we'd have to go to court, waste a lot of time and money, and end up with a big headache. You would too. Who wants that?

No, Mrs. Jones, we want to handle this problem fairly on the basis of some fair standard, rather than of power and selfish interest.

Analysis. Mrs. Jones challenges the idea of negotiating on the basis of principle, calling it a charade. It's a matter of will and her will is to throw out Turnbull and his roommate today.

At this Turnbull almost loses his temper — and with it his control over the negotiation. He feels like counterattacking: "I'd like to see you try to get us out. We'll go to court. We'll get your license revoked." The negotiation would then break off, and Turnbull would lose a lot of time, effort, and peace of mind. But instead of reacting, Turnbull keeps his temper and brings the negotiation back to the merits. This is a good example of negotiation jujitsu. He deflects Mrs. Jones's attack by taking responsibility for her mistaken perceptions, and he tries to persuade her of his sincere interest in principle. He does not hide either his selfish interests or his leverage over her; on the contrary, he makes both explicit. Once they are acknowledged, he can separate them from the merits and they can cease being an issue.

Turnbull also tries to give the game of principled negotiation some weight by telling Mrs. Jones this is his basic code — the way he always plays. He attributes this not to high-minded motives — which are always suspect — but to simple self-interest.

"Trust is a separate issue"

MRS. JONES: You don't trust me? After all I've done for you?
TURNBULL: Mrs. Jones, we appreciate all you've done for us. But trust isn't the issue here. The issue is the principle: Did we pay more than we should have? What considerations do you think we should take into account in deciding this?

Analysis. Mrs. Jones tries to manipulate Turnbull into a corner. Either he pursues the point and looks untrusting or he looks trusting and gives in. Turnbull slips out of the corner, however, by expressing his gratitude once more and then defining the question of trust as irrelevant. Turnbull at once reaffirms his appreciation of Mrs. Jones while he remains firm on the principle. Moreover, Turnbull does not just shunt aside the question of trust but actively directs the discussion back to principle by asking Mrs. Jones what considerations she thinks are relevant.

Turnbull sticks to principle without blaming Mrs. Jones. He never calls her dishonest. He does not ask, "Did you take advantage of us?" but inquires more impersonally, "Did we pay more than we should have?" Even if he does not trust her, it would be a poor strategy to tell her so. She would probably become defensive and angry and might either withdraw into a rigid position or break off the negotiation altogether.

It helps to have stock phrases like "It's not a question of trust" to turn aside ploys like Mrs. Jones's plea for trust.

"Could I ask you a few questions to see whether my facts are right?"

TURNBULL: Could I ask you a few questions to see whether the facts I've been given are right?

Is the apartment really under rent control?

Is the legal maximum rent really $233?

Paul asked me whether this makes us parties to a violation of law.

Did someone inform Paul at the time he signed the lease that the apartment was under rent control, and that the legal maximum was $67 lower than the rent he agreed to?

Analysis. Statements of fact can be threatening. Whenever you can, ask a question instead.

Turnbull might have declared, "The legal rent is $233. You broke the law. What's worse, you involved us in breaking the

law without telling us so." Mrs. Jones would probably have
reacted strongly to these statements, dismissing them as verbal
attacks intended to score points.

Phrasing each piece of information as a question allows
Mrs. Jones to participate, listen to the information, evaluate
it, and either accept or correct it. Turnbull communicates the
same information to her but in a less threatening manner. He
reduces the threat still further by attributing a particularly
pointed question to his absent roommate.

In effect, Turnbull induces Mrs. Jones to help lay a foundation of agreed-upon facts upon which a principled solution can
be built.

"What's the principle behind your action?"

TURNBULL: I'm not clear why you charged us $300 a month.
What were your reasons for charging that much?

Analysis. A principled negotiator neither accepts nor re-
jects the other side's positions. To keep the dialogue focused
on the merits, Turnbull questions Mrs. Jones about the reasons for her position. He does not ask whether there were any
reasons. He assumes there are good reasons. This flattering
assumption leads the other side to search for reasons even if
there are none, thus keeping the negotiation on the basis of
principle.

"Let me see if I understand what you're saying"

TURNBULL: Let me see if I understand what you're saying,
Mrs. Jones. If I've understood you correctly, you think the rent
we paid is fair because you made a lot of repairs and improvements to the apartment since the last rent control evaluation. It
wasn't worth your while to ask the Rent Control Board for an increase for the few months you rented the place to us.

In fact, you rented it only as a favor to Paul. And now you're concerned that we may take unfair advantage of you and try to get money from you as the price for moving out. Is there something I've missed or misunderstood?

Analysis. Principled negotiation requires good communication. Before responding to Mrs. Jones's arguments, Turnbull restates to her in positive terms what he has heard to make sure he has indeed understood her.

Once she feels understood, she can relax and discuss the problem constructively. She can't dismiss his arguments on the grounds that they do not take into account what she knows. She is likely to listen now and be more receptive. In trying to sum up her point of view, Turnbull establishes a cooperative game in which both are making sure he understands the facts.

"Let me get back to you"

TURNBULL: Now that I think I understand your point of view, let me talk with my roommate and explain it to him. Can I get back to you tomorrow sometime?

Analysis. A good negotiator rarely makes an important decision on the spot. The psychological pressure to be nice and to give in is too great. A little time and distance help separate the people from the problem.

A good negotiator comes to the table with a credible reason in his pocket for leaving when he wants. Such a reason should not indicate passivity or inability to make a decision. Here, Turnbull sounds as if he knows exactly what he is doing, and he arranges to resume the negotiation at a given time. He shows not only decisiveness but also control over the course of the negotiation.

Once away from the table, Turnbull can check on points of
information and consult his "constituency," Paul. He can think
about the decision and make sure he has not lost perspective.

Too much time at the table may wear down one's commitment to principled negotiation. Returning to the table with
renewed resolve, Turnbull can be soft on the person without
being soft on the problem.

"Let me show you where I have trouble following some of your reasoning"

TURNBULL: Let me show you where I have trouble following
some of your reasons for the extra $67 a month. One reason was
the repairs and improvements on the apartment. The Rent Control
Examiner said it would take about $10,000 in improvements to
justify an increase of $67 a month. How much money was spent
on improvements?

I must admit it didn't seem like $10,000 worth to Paul and me.
The hole in the linoleum you promised to repair was never fixed;
neither was the hole in the living room floor. The toilet broke
down repeatedly. These are just some of the defects and malfunc-
tions we found.

Analysis. In principled negotiation you should present all
your reasons first before offering a proposal. If principles come
afterwards, they appear not as the objective criteria which any
proposal should satisfy but as mere justifications for an arbitrary position.

For Turnbull to explain his reasons first shows his openness to persuasion and his awareness of the need to convince
Mrs. Jones. If he announced his proposal first, Mrs. Jones
probably would not bother to listen to the reasons that followed. Her mind would be elsewhere, considering what ob-
jections and counterproposals she could make.

"One fair solution might be . . . ."

TURNBULL: Given all the considerations we've discussed, one fair solution seems to be for Paul and me to be reimbursed for the amount of rent we paid in excess of the legal maximum. Does that sound fair to you?

Analysis. Turnbull presents a proposal not as *his,* but as a fair option which deserves their joint consideration. He does not claim it is the only fair solution, but *one* fair solution. He is specific without digging himself into a position and inviting rejection.

"If we agree . . . . If we disagree . . . ."

TURNBULL: If you and I could reach agreement now, Paul and I would move out immediately. If we can't reach an agreement, the hearing examiner at the Rent Control Board suggested that we stay in the apartment and withhold rent and/or sue you for reimbursement, treble damages, and legal fees. Paul and I are extremely reluctant to take either of these courses. We feel confident we can settle this matter fairly with you to your satisfaction and ours.

Analysis. Turnbull is trying to make it easy for Mrs. Jones to say yes to his proposal. So he starts by making it clear that all it takes for the problem to go away is Mrs. Jones's agreement.

The trickiest part of the message to communicate is the alternative if no agreement is reached. How can Turnbull get this across — he wants her to take it into account in her decision — without upsetting the negotiations? He bases the alternative on objective principle by attributing it to a legal authority — the hearing examiner. He distances himself personally from the suggestion. Nor does he say he will definitely take action. Instead, he leaves it as a possibility and emphasizes his reluctance to do anything drastic. Finally, he closes by affirming his confidence that a mutually satisfactory agreement will be reached.

Turnbull's BATNA — his best alternative to a negotiated agreement — is probably neither staying in the apartment nor going to court. He and Paul have already rented another apartment and would greatly prefer to move out now. A lawsuit would be difficult, given their busy schedules, and even if they won, they might never be able to collect. Turnbull's BATNA is probably just to move out and stop worrying about the $335 overpayment. Since his BATNA is probably less attractive than Mrs. Jones thinks, Turnbull does not disclose it.

"We'd be happy to see if we can leave when it's most convenient for you"

MRS. JONES: When do you plan to move out?

TURNBULL: As long as we've agreed on the appropriate rent for our time in the apartment, we'd be happy to see if we can leave when it's most convenient for you. When would you prefer?

Analysis. Sensing the possibility of a joint gain, Turnbull indicates his willingness to discuss ways of meeting Mrs. Jones's interest. As it turns out, Turnbull and Mrs. Jones have a shared interest in Turnbull moving out as soon as possible.

Incorporating her interests into the agreement not only gives her more of a stake in it but also allows Mrs. Jones to save face. On the one hand, she can feel good about agreeing to a fair solution even though it costs her money. On the other, she can say that she got the tenants out of the apartment early.

"It's been a pleasure dealing with you"

TURNBULL: Paul and I do appreciate, Mrs. Jones, all that you've done for us, and I'm pleased that we've settled this last problem fairly and amicably.

MRS. JONES: Thank you, Mr. Turnbull. Have a nice summer.

Analysis. Turnbull ends the negotiation on a final conciliatory note toward Mrs. Jones. Because they successfully dealt with the problem independently of the relationship, neither party feels cheated or angry, and neither is likely to try to sabotage or ignore their agreement. A working relationship is maintained for the future.

Whether you use principled negotiation and negotiation jujitsu, as Frank Turnbull did, or a third party with the one-text procedure, the conclusion remains the same: you *can* usually get the other side to play the game of principled negotiation with you, even if at first they appear unwilling.

8 | What If They Use Dirty Tricks?

(Taming the Hard Bargainer)

Principled negotiation is all very well, but what if the other negotiator deceives you or tries to throw you off balance? Or what if he escalates his demands just when you are on the verge of agreement?

There are many tactics and tricks people can use to try to take advantage of you. Everyone knows some of them. They range from lies and psychological abuse to various forms of pressure tactics. They may be illegal, unethical, or simply unpleasant. Their purpose is to help the user "win" some substantive gain in an unprincipled contest of will. Such tactics may be called tricky bargaining.

If they recognize that a tricky bargaining tactic is being used against them, most people respond in one of two ways. The first standard response is to put up with it. It is unpleasant to rock the boat. You may give the other side the benefit of the doubt or get angry and promise yourself never to deal with them again. For now, you hope for the best and keep quiet. Most people respond this way. They hope that if they give in this time, the other side will be appeased and will not ask for more. Sometimes this works, more often it fails. This is how Neville Chamberlain, the British Prime Minister, responded in 1938 to Hitler's negotiating tactics. After Chamberlain thought he had an agreement, Hitler raised his demands. At Munich, Chamberlain, hoping to avoid war, went along. A year later, World War II started.

The second common response is to respond in kind. If they start outrageously high, you start outrageously low. If they are deceptive, so are you. If they make threats, you make counterthreats. If they lock themselves into their position, you lock yourself even more tightly into yours. In the end either one party yields or, all too often, negotiation breaks off.

Such tricky tactics are illegitimate because they fail the test of reciprocity. They are designed to be used by only one side; the other side is not supposed to know the tactics or is expected to tolerate them knowingly. Earlier we argued that an effective counter to a one-sided substantive proposal is to examine the legitimacy of the principle that the proposal reflects. Tricky bargaining tactics are in effect one-sided proposals about negotiating *procedure*, about the negotiating game that the parties are going to play. To counter them, you will want to engage in principled negotiation about the negotiating process.

How do you negotiate about the rules of the game?

There are three steps in negotiating the rules of the negotiating game where the other side seems to be using a tricky tactic: recognize the tactic, raise the issue explicitly, and question the tactic's legitimacy and desirability — negotiate over it.

You have to know what is going on to be able to do something about it. Learn to spot particular ploys that indicate deception, those designed to make you uncomfortable, and those which lock the other side into their position. Often just recognizing a tactic will neutralize it. Realizing, for example, that the other side is attacking you personally in order to impair your judgment may well frustrate the effort.

After recognizing the tactic, bring it up with the other side. "Say, Joe, I may be totally mistaken, but I'm getting the feeling that you and Ted here are playing a good-guy/bad-guy routine. If you two want a recess any time to straighten out differences between you, just ask." Discussing the tactic not only makes it less effective, it also may cause the other side to worry about alienating you completely. Simply raising a question about a tactic may be enough to get them to stop using it.

The most important purpose of bringing the tactic up explicitly, however, is to give you an opportunity to negotiate about the rules of the game. This is the third step. This negotiation focuses on procedure instead of substance, but the goal remains to produce a wise agreement (this time about procedure) efficiently and amicably. Not surprisingly, the method remains the same.

Separate the people from the problem. Don't attack people personally for using a tactic you consider illegitimate. If they get defensive it may be more difficult for them to give up the tactic, and they may be left with a residue of anger that will fester and interfere with other issues. Question the tactic, not their personal integrity. Rather than saying, "You deliberately put me here facing the sun," attack the problem: "I am finding the sun in my eyes quite distracting. Unless we can solve that problem, I may have to leave early to get some rest. Shall we revise the schedule?" It will be easier to reform the negotiating process than to reform those with whom you are dealing. Don't be diverted from the negotiation by the urge to teach them a lesson.

Focus on interests, not positions. "Why are you committing yourself in the press to an extreme position? Are you trying to protect yourself from criticism? Or are you protecting yourself from changing your position? Is it in our mutual interest to have both of us use this tactic?"

Invent options for mutual gain. Suggest alternative games to play. "How about our undertaking to make no statements to the press until we reach agreement or break off the talks?"

Insist on objective criteria. Above all, be hard on principle. "Is there a theory behind having me sit in the low chair with my back to the open door?" Try out the principle of reciprocity on them. "I assume that you will sit in this chair tomorrow morning?" Frame the principle behind each tactic as a proposed "rule" for the game. "Shall we alternate spilling coffee on one another day by day?"

As a last resort, turn to your BATNA (your Best Alternative To a Negotiated Agreement) and walk out. "It's my impression that you're not interested in negotiating in a way that we both think will produce results. Here's my phone number. If I'm mistaken, I'm ready any time you are. Until then, we'll pursue the court option." If you are walking out on clearly legitimate grounds, as when they have deliberately deceived you about facts or their authority, and if they are genuinely interested in an agreement, they are likely to call you back to the table.

Some common tricky tactics

Tricky tactics can be divided into three categories: deliberate deception, psychological warfare, and positional pressure tactics. You should be prepared to deal with all three. Below are a number of common examples of each type; for each in turn, we show how principled negotiation might be applied to counter it.

Deliberate deception

Perhaps the most common form of dirty trick is misrepresentation about facts, authority, or intentions.

Phony facts. The oldest form of negotiating trickery is to make some knowingly false statement: "This car was driven only 5,000 miles by a little old lady from Pasadena who never went over 35 miles per hour." The dangers of being taken in by false statements are great. What can you do?

Separate the people from the problem. Unless you have good reason to trust somebody, don't. This does not mean calling him a liar; rather it means making the negotiation proceed independent of trust. Do not let someone treat your doubts as a personal attack. No seller is likely to give you a watch or a car simply in exchange for your statement that you have money in the bank. Just as a seller will routinely check on your credit ("because there are so many other people around that can't be trusted"), you can do the same for statements of the other side. A practice of verifying factual assertions reduces the incentive for deception, and your risk of being cheated.

Ambiguous authority. The other side may allow you to believe that they, like you, have full authority to compromise when they don't. After they have pressed you as hard as they can and you have worked out what you believe to be a firm agreement, they announce that they must take it to someone else for approval. This technique is designed to give them a "second bite at the apple."

This is a bad situation to fall into. If only *you* have authority to make concessions, only you will make concessions.

Do not assume that the other side has full authority just because they are there negotiating with you. An insurance adjuster, a lawyer, or a salesman may allow you to think that your flexibility is being matched by flexibility on their side. You may later find that what you thought was an agreement will be treated by the other side as simply a floor for further negotiation.

Before starting on any give-and-take, find out about the authority of the other side. It is perfectly legitimate to inquire,

"Just how much authority do you have in this particular negotiation?" If the answer is ambiguous, you may wish to talk to someone with real authority or to make clear that you on your side are reserving equal freedom to reconsider any point.

If they do announce unexpectedly that they are treating what you thought was an agreement as a basis for further negotiation, insist on reciprocity. "All right. We will treat it as a joint draft to which neither side is committed. You check with your boss and I'll sleep on it and see if I come up with any changes I want to suggest tomorrow." Or you might say, "If your boss approves this draft tomorrow, I'll stick by it. Otherwise each of us should feel free to propose changes."

Dubious intentions. Where the issue is one of possible misrepresentation of their intention to comply with the agreement, it is often possible to build compliance features into the agreement itself.

Suppose you are a lawyer representing the wife in a divorce negotiation. Your client does not believe her husband will pay child support even though he may agree to do so. The time and energy spent in going to court every month may make her give up the effort. What can you do? Make the problem explicit and use their protestations to get a guarantee. You could say to the husband's lawyer, "Look, my client is afraid those child support payments simply aren't going to be made. Rather than monthly payments, how about giving her equity in the house?" The husband's lawyer may say, "My client is perfectly trustworthy. We'll put it in writing that he will pay child support regularly." To which you might respond, "It's not a matter of trust. Are you certain that your client will pay?"

"Of course."

"A hundred percent certain?"

"Yes, I'm a hundred percent certain."

"Then you won't mind a contingent agreement. Your client

will agree to make child support payments. We'll provide that if, for some inexplicable reason which you estimate at zero percent probability, he misses two payments, my client will get the equity in the house (minus of course the amount your client has already paid out in child support) and your client will no longer be liable for child support." It is not easy for the husband's lawyer to object.

Less than full disclosure is not the same as deception. Deliberate deception as to facts or one's intentions is quite different from not fully disclosing one's present thinking. Good faith negotiation does not require total disclosure. Perhaps the best answer to questions such as "What is the most you would pay if you had to?" would be along the following lines: "Let's not put ourselves under such a strong temptation to mislead. If you think no agreement is possible, and that we may be wasting our time, perhaps we could disclose our thinking to some trustworthy third party, who can then tell us whether there is a zone of potential agreement." In this way it is possible to behave with full candor about information that is not being disclosed.

Psychological warfare

These tactics are designed to make you feel uncomfortable, so that you will have a subconscious desire to end the negotiation as soon as possible.

Stressful situations. Much has been written about the physical circumstances in which negotiations take place. You should be sensitive to such modest questions as whether a meeting takes place at your place or theirs, or on neutral territory. Contrary to the accepted wisdom, it is sometimes advantageous to accept an offer to meet on the other side's turf. It may put them at ease, making them more open to your suggestions. If necessary, it will be easier for you to walk out. If, however, you do allow the other side to choose the physical environment, be aware of what that choice is and what effects it may have.

Ask yourself if you feel under stress, and if so, why. If the room is too noisy, if the temperature is too hot or cold, if there is no place for a private caucus with a colleague, be aware that the setting might have been deliberately designed to make you want to conclude negotiations promptly and, if necessary, to yield points in order to do so.

If you find the physical surroundings prejudicial, do not hesitate to say so. You can suggest changing chairs, taking a break, or adjourning to a different location or another time. In every case your job is to identify the problem, be willing to raise it with the other side, and then negotiate better physical circumstances in an objective and principled fashion.

Personal attacks. In addition to manipulating the physical environment, there are also ways for the other side to use verbal and nonverbal communication to make you feel uncomfortable. They can comment on your clothes or your appearance. "Looks like you were up all night. Things not going well at the office?" They can attack your status by making you wait for them or by interrupting the negotiations to deal with other people. They can imply that you are ignorant. They can refuse to listen to you and make you repeat yourself. They can deliberately refuse to make eye contact with you. (Simple experiments with students have confirmed the malaise many feel when this tactic is used; and they are unable to identify the cause of the problem.) In each case recognizing the tactic will help nullify its effect; bringing it up explicitly will probably prevent a recurrence.

The good-guy/bad-guy routine. One form of psychological pressure which also involves deception is the good-guy/bad-guy routine. This technique appears in its starkest form in old police movies. The first policeman threatens the suspect with prosecution for numerous crimes, puts him under a bright

light, pushes him around, then finally takes a break and leaves.
The good guy then turns off the light, offers the suspect a
cigarette, and apologizes for the tough policeman. He says
he'd like to control the tough guy, but he can't unless the suspect cooperates. The result: the suspect tells all he knows.

Similarly in a negotiation, two people on the same side will
stage a quarrel. One will take a tough stand: "These books
cost $4,000, and I won't accept a penny less." His partner
looks pained and a little embarrassed. Finally he breaks in:
"Frank, you are being unreasonable. After all, these books are
two years old, even if they haven't been used much." Turning
to the other side, he says reasonably, "Could you pay $3,800?"
The concession isn't large, but it almost seems like a favor.

The good-guy/bad-guy routine is a form of psychological
manipulation. If you recognize it, you won't be taken in. When
the good guy makes his pitch, just ask him the same question
you asked the bad guy: "I appreciate that you are trying to
be reasonable, but I still want to know why you think that's
a fair price. What is your principle? I am willing to accept
$4,000 if you can persuade me it's the fairest price."

Threats. Threats are one of the most abused tactics in
negotiation. A threat seems easy to make — much easier than
an offer. All it takes is a few words, and if it works, you never
have to carry it out. But threats can lead to counterthreats in
an escalating spiral that can unhinge a negotiation and even
destroy a relationship.

Threats are pressure. Pressure often accomplishes just the
opposite of what it is intended to do; it builds up pressure the
other way. Instead of making a decision easier for the other
side, it often makes it more difficult. In response to outside
pressure, a union, a committee, a company, or a government
may close ranks. Moderates and hawks join together to resist
what they may perceive as an illegitimate attempt to coerce
them. The question changes from "Should we make this decision?" to "Shall we cave in to outside pressure?"

Good negotiators rarely resort to threats. They do not need to; there are other ways to communicate the same information. If it seems appropriate to outline the consequences of the other side's action, suggest those that will occur independently of your will rather than those you could choose to bring about. *Warnings* are much more legitimate than threats and are not vulnerable to counterthreats: "Should we fail to reach agreement, it seems highly probable to me that the news media would insist on publishing the whole sordid story. In a matter of this much public interest, I don't see how we could legitimately suppress information. Do you?"

For threats to be effective they must be credibly communicated. Sometimes you can interfere with the communication process. You can ignore threats; you can take them as unauthorized, spoken in haste, or simply irrelevant. You can also make it risky to communicate them. At a coal mine where one of the authors was recently mediating, a large number of false but costly bomb threats were being received. These dropped off dramatically when the company's receptionist began answering all phone calls with "Your voice is being recorded. What number are you calling?"

Sometimes threats can be turned to your political advantage. A union could announce to the press: "Management has such a weak case that they are resorting to threats." Perhaps the best response to a threat, however, is to be principled. "We have prepared a sequence of countermoves for each of management's customary threats. However, we have delayed taking action until we see whether we can agree that making threats is not the most constructive activity we could engage in just now." Or "I only negotiate on the merits. My reputation is built on not responding to threats."

Positional pressure tactics
This kind of bargaining tactic is designed to structure the

situation so that only one side can effectively make concessions.

Refusal to negotiate. When the American diplomats and
embassy personnel were taken hostage in Tehran in November 1979, the Iranian government announced its demands and
refused to negotiate. A lawyer will often do the same, simply
telling opposing counsel, "I'll see you in court." What can you
do when the other side refuses to negotiate altogether?

First, recognize the tactic as a possible negotiating ploy: an
attempt to use their entry into negotiation as a bargaining chip
to obtain some concession on substance. A variant on this ploy
is to set preconditions for negotiations.

Second, talk about their refusal to negotiate. Communicate
either directly or through third parties. Don't attack them
for refusing to negotiate, but rather find out their interests in
not negotiating. Are they worried about giving you status by
talking to you? Will those who talk with you be criticized for
being "soft"? Do they think negotiation will destroy their precarious internal unity? Or do they simply not believe that an
agreement is possible?

Suggest some options, such as negotiating through third
parties, sending letters, or encouraging private individuals like
journalists to discuss the issues (as happened in the Iranian
case).

Finally, insist on principles. Is this the way they would want
you to play? Do they want you to set preconditions as well?
Will they want others to refuse to negotiate with them? What
are the principles they think should apply to this situation?

Extreme demands. Negotiators will frequently start with
extreme proposals like offering $25,000 for your house which
is apparently worth $100,000. The goal is to lower your ex-
pectations. They also figure that an extreme initial position
will give them a better end result, on the theory that the parties will ultimately end up splitting the difference between

their positions. There are drawbacks to this approach, even for tricky bargainers. Making an extreme demand that both you and they know will be abandoned undermines their credibility. Such an opening may also kill the deal; if they offer too little, you may think they are not worth bothering with.

Bringing the tactic to their attention works well here. Ask for principled justification of their position until it looks ridiculous even to them.

Escalating demands. A negotiator may raise one of his demands for every concession he makes on another. He may also reopen issues you thought had been settled. The benefits of this tactic lie in decreasing the overall concession, and in the psychological effect of making you want to agree quickly before he raises any more of his demands.

The Prime Minister of Malta used this tactic in negotiating with Great Britain in 1971 over the price of naval and air base rights. Each time the British thought they had an agreement, he would say, "Yes, agreed, but there is still one small problem." And the small problem would turn out to be a £10 million cash advance or guaranteed jobs for dockyard and base workers for the life of the contract.

When you recognize this, call it to their attention and then perhaps take a break while you consider whether and on what basis you want to continue negotiations. This avoids an impulsive reaction while indicating the seriousness of their conduct. And again, insist on principle. When you come back, anyone interested in settlement will be more serious.

Lock-in tactics. This tactic is illustrated by Thomas Schelling's well-known example of two dynamite trucks barreling toward each other on a single-lane road. The question becomes which truck goes off the road to avoid an accident. As the trucks near each other, one driver in full view of the other pulls off his steering wheel and throws it out the window. Seeing this, the other driver has a choice between an explosive crash or driving his truck off the road into a ditch. This is an example of an extreme commitment tactic designed to make it impossible to yield. Paradoxically, you strengthen your bargaining position by weakening your control over the situation.

In labor-management and international negotiations this tactic is common. A union president makes a rousing speech to his constituency pledging that he will never accept less than a 15 percent salary increase. Since he stands to lose face and credibility if he does agree to anything less, he can more convincingly persuade management the union must have 15 percent.

But lock-in tactics are gambles. You may call the other side's bluff and force them to make a concession which they will then have to explain to their constituency.

Like threats, lock-in tactics depend on communication. If the other truck driver does not see the steering wheel fly out the window, or if he thinks the truck has an emergency steering mechanism, the act of throwing the steering wheel out the window will not have its intended effect. The pressure to avoid a collision will be felt equally by both drivers.

In response to a commitment tactic, therefore, you may be able to interrupt the communication. You can so interpret the commitment as to weaken it. "Oh I see. You told the papers your *goal* was to settle for $200,000. Well, we all have our aspirations, I guess. Do you want to know what mine are?" Alternatively, you can crack a joke and not take the lock-in seriously.

You can also resist lock-ins on principle: "Fine, Bob, I understand you made that statement publicly. But my practice is never to yield to pressure, only to reason. Now let's talk about the merits of the problem." Whatever you do, avoid making the commitment a central question. Deemphasize it so that the other side can more gracefully back down.

Hardhearted partner. Perhaps the most common negotiating tactic used to justify not yielding to your requests is for the other negotiator to say that he personally would have no objection but his hardhearted partner will not let him. "It's a perfectly reasonable request, I agree. But my wife absolutely refuses to go along with me on it."

Recognize the tactic. Rather than discussing it with the other negotiator, you may want to get his agreement to the principle involved — perhaps in writing — and then if possible speak directly with the "hardhearted partner."

A calculated delay. Frequently one side will try to postpone coming to a decision until a time they think favorable. Labor negotiators will often delay until the last few hours before a strike deadline, relying on the psychological pressure of the deadline to make management more malleable. Unfortunately, they often miscalculate and the strike deadline passes. Once the strike begins, management, in turn, may decide to wait for a more favorable time, such as when the union's strike fund has run out. Waiting for the right time is a high-cost game.

In addition to making delaying tactics explicit and negotiating about them, consider creating a fading opportunity for the other side. If you represent one company negotiating a merger with another, start talks with a third company, exploring the possibility of merging with them instead. Look for objective conditions that can be used to establish deadlines, such as the date on which taxes are due, the annual trustees meeting, the end of the contract, or the end of the legislative session.

"Take it or leave it." There is nothing inherently wrong with confronting the other side with a firm choice. In fact, most American business is conducted this way. If you go into a supermarket and see a can of beans marked 59 cents, you don't try to negotiate with the supermarket manager. This is

an efficient method of conducting business, but it is not negotiation. It is not interactive decision-making. Nor is there
anything wrong after long negotiations to conclude them when
you mean to do so by saying, "Take it or leave it," except
that you should probably phrase it more politely.

As an alternative to explicitly recognizing the "Take it or
leave it" tactic and negotiating about it, consider ignoring it
at first. Keep talking as if you didn't hear it, or change the
subject, perhaps by introducing other solutions. If you do
bring up the tactic specifically, let them know what they have
to lose if no agreement is reached and look for a face-saving
way, such as a change in circumstances, for them to get out
of the situation. After management has announced its final
offer, the union could tell them, "A $1.69 raise was your final
offer before we discussed our cooperative efforts to make the
plant more productive."

Don't be a victim
It is often hard to decide what it means to negotiate in "good
faith." People draw the line in different places. It may help to
ask yourself such questions as: Is this an approach I would
use in dealing with a good friend or a member of my family?
If a full account of what I said and did appeared in the news-
papers, would I be embarrassed? In literature, would such
conduct be more appropriate for a hero or a villain? These
questions are not intended to bring external opinion to bear
so much as to shed light on your own internal values. You
must decide on your own whether you want to use tactics
you would consider improper and in bad faith if used against
you.

It may be useful at the beginning of the negotiation to say,
"Look, I know this may be unusual, but I want to know the
rules of the game we're going to play. Are we both trying to

reach a wise agreement as quickly and with as little effort as possible? Or are we going to play 'hard bargaining' where the more stubborn fellow wins?" Whatever you do, be prepared to fight dirty bargaining tactics. You can be just as firm as they can, even firmer. It is easier to defend principle than an illegitimate tactic.

IV | In Conclusion

In Conclusion

Three points.

You knew it all the time

There is probably nothing in this book which you did not already know at some level of your experience. What we have tried to do is to organize common sense and common experience in a way that provides a usable framework for thinking and acting. The more consistent these ideas are with your knowledge and intuition the better. In teaching this method to skilled lawyers and businessmen with years of experience, we have been told, "Now I know what I have been doing, and why it sometimes works" and "I knew what you were saying was right because I knew it already."

Learn from doing

A book can point you in a promising direction. By making you aware of ideas and aware of what you are doing, it can help you learn.

No one, however, can make you skillful but yourself. Reading the pamphlet on the Royal Canadian Air Force exercises will not make you physically fit. Studying books on tennis, swimming, riding a bicycle, or riding a horse will not make you an expert. Negotiation is no different.

"Winning"

In 1964 an American father and his twelve-year-old son were enjoying a beautiful Saturday in Hyde Park, London, playing catch with a Frisbee. Few in England had seen a Frisbee at that time and a small group of strollers gathered to watch this strange sport. Finally, one Homburg-clad Britisher came over to the father: "Sorry to bother you. Been watching you a quarter of an hour. Who's *winning?*"

In most instances to ask a negotiator, "Who's winning?" is as inappropriate as to ask who's winning a marriage. If you ask that question about your marriage, you have already lost the more important negotiation — the one about what kind of game to play, about the way you deal with each other and your shared and differing interests.

This book is about how to "win" that important game — how to achieve a better process for dealing with your differences. To be better, the process must, of course, produce good substantive results; winning on the merits may not be the only goal, but certainly losing is not the answer. Both theory and experience suggest that the method of principled negotiation will produce over the long run substantive outcomes as good as or better than you are likely to obtain using any other negotiation strategy. In addition, it should prove more efficient and less costly to human relationships. We find the method comfortable to use and hope you will too.

That does not mean it is easy to change habits, to disentangle emotions from the merits, or to enlist others in the task of working out a wise solution to a shared problem. From time to time you may want to remind yourself that the first thing you are trying to win is a better way to negotiate — a way that avoids your having to choose between the satisfactions of getting what you deserve and of being decent. You can have both.

Analytical Table of Contents

III. YES, BUT . . .

IV. IN CONCLUSION

A Note on the Harvard Negotiation Project

The Harvard Negotiation Project is a research project at Harvard University which works on negotiation problems and develops and disseminates improved methods of negotiation and mediation. The Project's activities include:

Theory building. The Project has developed such ideas as the one-text mediation procedure used by the United States in the Middle East peace negotiations at Camp David in September 1978, and the method of principled negotiation summarized in this book. The Project hosts — and members of the Project participate in — the meetings of the Negotiation Seminar, a loose consortium of scholars at Harvard, MIT, and Tufts working on negotiation theory.

Education and training. The Project develops programs for professionals (lawyers, businessmen, diplomats, journalists, government officials, union leaders, military officers, and others), and is working on courses for university and high school students.

Publications. The Project is preparing practical materials such as *International Mediation: A Working Guide* (now in a draft edition), a check list for negotiators, case studies, and forms designed to be of use to practitioners and students.

Conflict clinic. Participants in ongoing conflicts, international and domestic, are sometimes invited to the Project so that Project members (and participants themselves) may learn more about the negotiation process.